The Grand Mage Wars: The Battle of Legends Unfold

Myrddin Sage

Published by Myrddin Sage, 2024.

While every precaution has been taken in the preparation of this book, the publisher assumes no responsibility for errors or omissions, or for damages resulting from the use of the information contained herein.

THE GRAND MAGE WARS: THE BATTLE OF LEGENDS UNFOLD

First edition. November 7, 2024.

Copyright © 2024 Myrddin Sage.

ISBN: 979-8227641229

Written by Myrddin Sage.

Table of Contents

The Grand Mage Wars: The Battle of Legends Unfold 1

Preface 2

Chapter 1: Whispers of Legends Reborn 4

Chapter 2: Echoes of Universal Strife 14

Chapter 3: Depths of Character 25

Chapter 4: Arcane Realms of Reason 35

Chapter 5: The Dynamic Reader's Role 46

Chapter 6: The Unforeseen Magic 55

Chapter 7: Emotional Landscapes Unveiled 65

Chapter 8: Through the Lens of Legacy 76

Epilogue 86

Dedication

To all those who believe in the magic within themselves,

This book is dedicated to the dreamers, the warriors, and the legends in their own right. May the tales of courage, sorcery, and epic battles within these pages inspire you to unleash the grand mage within and embrace the battles that unfold in the quest for your own legendary destiny.

Epigraph

"In the heart of every legend lies a battle unfought and a hero unsung. Step into the shadows, embrace the magic, and let your story be written in the stars." - **Unknown.**

The Grand Mage Wars: The Battle of Legends Unfold

Dive Into an Ancient Conflict with Merlin and Morganna, Where Magic Meets Myth in a Captivating Tale

Preface

"*Magic is believing in yourself; if you can do that, you can make anything happen.*" - Johann Wolfgang von Goethe.

In the luminous folds of fantasy and the shadowy corners of ancient lore, the tale of **"The Grand Mage Wars: The Battle of Legends Unfold"** emerges as a beacon for those who seek to lose themselves in a world where magic intertwines with myth. This book is crafted not merely as a narrative but as an exploration into the depths of magical warfare, where the legendary figures of Merlin and Morganna wage a war that is as much about wits and wisdom as it is about spells and sorcery.

The essence of this story is rooted in the classic struggle between good and evil but with a twist that delves into the complexities of power, loyalty, and the human (*or not-so-human*) spirit. The purpose behind weaving such a tale was to offer a fresh perspective on timeless characters while engaging and thrilling readers with new adventures and unexpected alliances.

I was inspired to write this book by those moments of quiet contemplation when the lines between reality and fantasy blur, where you find yourself rooting for heroes that exist in the echoes of ancient tales. I've spoken with many who still seek that thrill—the excitement of watching magnificent powers clash and the suspense of complex strategies unfolding. Reflecting on our shared hunger for epic narratives led me to craft a world that feels both familiar and thrillingly novel.

THE GRAND MAGE WARS: THE BATTLE OF LEGENDS UNFOLD

Throughout the writing process, I've been buoyed by the works of classic fantasy authors and modern myth-makers. These authors have spun worlds out of words and woven tapestries of immense narrative depth. Their stories prompted me to push traditional magic lore's boundaries, integrating the known and the unknown into a single, compelling narrative.

A heartfelt thank you extends to everyone who supported this endeavor—from those who provided their insights into the lore that inspired it to friends and family who bore with my endless discussions about character motives and magical laws. But most importantly, my gratitude goes out to you, the reader, for choosing to embark on this journey through pages filled with enchantment and conflict.

This book is specially crafted for those who cherish not just any fantasy but a fantasy that brings together elements of classical mythology with sparks of new invention. Whether you are a young adult or someone who has kept the child alive, if you revel in the escapism offered by vivid battles and intricate character dynamics, then this is your gateway to an extraordinary world.

As you turn these pages, let yourself be transported into the tumultuous yet mesmerizing conflicts between powerful mages and their legendary creatures. Feel the ground shake under dragons' feet and smell the singed air in the aftermath of a spell duel. Hear the whispers of ancient woods where mythical beings concoct their plans. This isn't just a story; it's an experience—a magical quest I invite you to join.

Thank you for your trust in my words and words. I am excited for you to uncover the secrets and witness the legends as they unfold. Let's begin this enchanting journey together!

Chapter 1: Whispers of Legends Reborn

Can Old Myths Forge New Realities?

In the dim glow of twilight, Arthur Pendragon stood at the edge of his grandfather's estate, overlooking a field that stretched towards the horizon like a green sea. His eyes, reflecting the sky's deepening blue, scanned the landscape as if searching for answers hidden beneath the earth. He had returned to this ancestral home not out of nostalgia but driven by a curious blend of duty and ambition.

Arthur had recently inherited this land and an ancient library filled with manuscripts and tomes about legendary figures like Merlin and Morganna. These stories whispered to him from the past, urging him to blend these ancient myths with his modern designs.

He envisioned creating a series of graphic novels that would breathe new life into these tales, combining them with fresh elements and creatures never seen in his family's narratives.

His boots crunched on the gravel path as he returned to the house.

The air was crisp, carrying scents of moss and damp soil mixed with the distant aroma of woodsmoke from the chimney. Inside, the library awaited him—a sanctuary lined with old books. He traced his fingers over the spines, feeling their leather-bound histories pulse under his touch.

Arthur settled into a high-backed chair beside a large window where light pooled on an open page. He pondered how to intertwine well-known legends with newly imagined elements without betraying their original essence. The challenge wasn't just artistic; it was deeply personal. His grandmother often told him tales where magic was not just fantasy but reality's undercurrent.

The room grew darker as night fell; only his desk lamp illuminated the sketches and notes scattered before him. Outside, an owl hooted—a sound that seemed ancient and immediate. It reminded Arthur that he was not just creating stories; he was reviving lore so it could enchant anew.

How can one honor tradition while boldly forging into uncharted narrative territories?

Reawakening the Ancient Magic: A New Dawn in Fantasy

The realm of fantasy literature has long been a sanctuary for those enchanted by the mystical and the mythical. As we embark on this literary journey through *"The Grand Mage Wars: The Battle of Legends Unfold,"* we rekindle our acquaintance with legendary figures like Merlin and Morganna while simultaneously venturing into uncharted territories adorned with newly conceived myths and fantastical creatures. This opening chapter, *"Whispers of Legends Reborn,"* promises to lay a robust foundation, merging the familiar echoes of traditional fantasy with innovative elements that revitalize the genre.

Rediscovering Timeless Magic

At its core, this chapter reintroduces ***classic fantasy elements*** that have captivated audiences for generations. Characters like Merlin have become almost archetypal within Western culture, embodying wisdom and power intertwined with a deep moral complexity. By bringing these characters back to the forefront, the narrative offers a comforting touchstone for longtime fans of the genre. However, it's not merely about nostalgia; it's about setting the stage for a deeper exploration and expansion of these characters beyond their conventional portrayals.

Embracing Novelty within Tradition

Parallel to revisiting familiar legends, this chapter begins to weave in **new mythical creatures and environments**, enriching the tapestry of the story. These elements are pivotal not just for their novelty but also for their role in advancing the plot and deepening the saga's thematic concerns. Introducing new creatures and magic systems inject freshness into the tale, offering new lore for readers to delve into, thereby expanding the universe in complexity and appeal.

Balancing Old and New

How does this blend of old and new influence reader engagement? This synthesis allows for a dual satisfaction: veteran enthusiasts appreciate the homage to known legends, while newcomers find allure in innovative storytelling and world-building. This strategic fusion is designed to broaden the narrative's appeal, attracting a diverse audience whose collective curiosity is piqued by different facets of the fantasy realm.

Previewing Themes and Conflicts

As we progress through this opening chapter, it's clear that the overarching themes of *conflict, power, and legacy* will be pivotal throughout *"The Grand Mage Wars."* The historic rivalry between Merlin and Morganna serves as more than just a backdrop; it's a dynamic catalyst driving the narrative forward, challenging characters and readers alike to reconsider notions of right, wrong, and everything in between.

Engaging with Depth and Complexity

This book doesn't just aim to entertain; it invites readers into a profound dialogue with its content. By engaging with this revived world where ancient magics stir once again amidst modern innovations, readers are prompted to reflect on how past narratives shape our understanding of new ones. This reflective quality ensures that *"The Grand Mage Wars"* is absorbing and intellectually stimulating.

CONCLUSION: SETTING the Stage

In summary, *"Whispers of Legends Reborn"* sets a promising stage for loyal fans and newcomers. Through adept reintroducing classic fantasy elements alongside fresh mythological innovations, it crafts a narrative deeply rooted in tradition and boldly forward-looking.

As we turn each page, we find ourselves drawn deeper into a world where every whisper of legend promises new discoveries, ensuring that our journey through *"The Grand Mage Wars"* will be as enchanting as it is enlightening.

In *"The Grand Mage Wars,"* classic fantasy elements are skillfully reintroduced, blending familiarity with innovation to create a rich, captivating narrative that appeals to a broad audience. The story revisits well-known characters such as Merlin and Morganna, drawing on the allure of ancient legends to immerse readers in a world of magic and mystique. By incorporating these iconic figures, the narrative taps into nostalgia for traditional fantasy tales while offering a fresh perspective that keeps the storyline engaging and unpredictable.

Magic and Mystery: One key classic fantasy element reintroduced in the narrative is the concept of magic as a powerful force that shapes the world and its inhabitants. From enchanting spells to mystical artifacts, magic plays a central role in driving the plot forward and adding an element of wonder to the story. Readers are transported to a realm where the impossible becomes possible, wizards weave intricate spells, and mythical creatures roam free.

This return to the core essence of magic in fantasy storytelling evokes a sense of awe and fascination, inviting readers to suspend their disbelief and embrace the fantastical.

Epic Quests and Heroic Journeys: Another classic element woven into the narrative is the theme of epic quests and heroic journeys undertaken by brave protagonists. As characters navigate treacherous landscapes, confront formidable foes, and overcome seemingly insurmountable challenges, readers are swept along on a thrilling adventure filled with twists and turns. The allure of embarking on a quest for truth, justice, or redemption resonates deeply with audiences, tapping into universal themes of courage, sacrifice, and triumph against all odds.

Legendary Creatures and Beings: A third classic fantasy element reintroduced in the narrative is the presence of legendary creatures and beings that populate the mystical world of *"The Grand Mage Wars."* From majestic dragons to elusive faeries, these fantastical entities add depth and intrigue to the story, infusing it with a sense of wonder and enchantment. Through encounters with these mythical creatures, readers are transported to a realm where imagination knows no bounds, where every corner holds the promise of encountering something extraordinary.

Continue reading to discover how new mythical creatures are seamlessly integrated into this captivating tale.

In *"The Grand Mage Wars,"* the integration of new mythical creatures adds a layer of intrigue and excitement to the narrative, enhancing the classic fantasy elements with fresh perspectives.

THE GRAND MAGE WARS: THE BATTLE OF LEGENDS UNFOLD

These new creatures bring a dynamic element to the story, introducing readers to fantastical beings that spark the imagination and broaden the scope of the magical world within the book. From majestic dragons soaring across the skies to elusive forest spirits that whisper secrets in ancient groves, each creature contributes to the rich tapestry of myths and legends woven throughout the tale.

One of the most impactful aspects of these new mythical creatures is their ability to challenge traditional perceptions and assumptions about fantasy beings. The story delves into complex themes of identity, power, and destiny by introducing unique characteristics and motivations for these creatures. Readers are invited to explore these creatures as magical entities and nuanced individuals with their own stories to tell.

The presence of these new mythical creatures also drives the plot forward, creating obstacles and alliances that shape the course of events in unexpected ways. Whether aiding the protagonists on their quest or hindering their progress, each creature plays a crucial role in shaping the outcome of the grand conflict at the heart of the story. *Their impact on the narrative is profound*, adding layers of depth and complexity that keep readers engaged and eager to uncover more about these captivating beings.

Furthermore, these new creatures offer a fresh perspective on familiar themes, challenging preconceived notions and inviting readers to reconsider their understanding of magic and myth. By blending classic fantasy elements with innovative twists, "The Grand Mage Wars" presents a world that is both comforting in its familiarity and exhilarating in its novelty. *This fusion of old and new creates a vibrant tapestry of wonder and excitement* that captivates readers from start to finish.

As readers delve deeper into the realm of these new mythical creatures, they are encouraged to embrace curiosity and open-mindedness, allowing themselves to be swept away by the magic and mystery that unfolds before them. Each encounter with these fantastical beings offers a glimpse into a world where anything is possible, where legends come to life in dazzling detail.

Ultimately, the integration of new mythical creatures in "The Grand Mage Wars" is a testament to the power of imagination.

By daring to dream up new beings with unique abilities and characteristics, the story invites readers to explore realms beyond their wildest fantasies, encouraging them to believe in the extraordinary possibilities beyond the veil of reality. In this enchanted world where myths reign supreme, every creature tells a story waiting to be discovered, inviting readers on an unforgettable journey through realms of magic and wonder.

Blending old and new elements in a narrative is like crafting a timeless recipe with a modern twist. In *"The Grand Mage Wars,"* this fusion of classic fantasy elements with innovative mythical creatures creates a rich tapestry that appeals to a broad readership.

The story balances nostalgia and excitement by intertwining familiar legends like Merlin and Morganna with fresh, imaginative beings, drawing in both traditional fantasy enthusiasts and those seeking something new.

The infusion of classic characters such as Merlin brings comfort and recognition to readers who have grown up with tales of legendary wizards. These figures carry a weight of history and mythos that immediately grounds the story in a familiar landscape, inviting readers to explore the narrative and anticipate what these iconic characters will bring to the tale.

On the other hand, introducing new mythical creatures injects an element of surprise and curiosity into the mix. These innovative beings add layers of complexity to the world-building, offering fresh challenges and dynamics for the characters to navigate. They catalyze change and growth, keeping the narrative engaging and unpredictable.

Combining old and new elements, "The Grand Mage Wars" offers a unique reading experience that caters to different tastes within the fantasy genre. For those who cherish the classics, seeing familiar faces woven into a new narrative tapestry evokes a sense of homage and reverence. Simultaneously, for readers craving innovation and evolution in their storytelling, introducing novel creatures brings fresh air, sparking imagination and wonder.

This blend satisfies existing fans by honoring beloved legends. It attracts newcomers drawn to the promise of a harmonious blend of tradition and innovation. The interplay between old and new elements creates a dynamic storytelling environment where expectations are subverted, conventions are challenged, and readers are taken on an immersive journey that transcends conventional boundaries.

In essence, blending old and new elements is like creating a bridge between generations of storytelling. It honors the past while embracing the future, creating a narrative space where diverse readers can find common ground and shared excitement. This fusion speaks to the universal appeal of fantasy literature—the timeless allure of ancient myths intertwined with the ever-evolving landscape of imagination.

Ultimately, by seamlessly weaving classic fantasy elements together with fresh mythical creatures, *"The Grand Mage Wars"* strikes a delicate balance that resonates with seasoned fantasy enthusiasts and newcomers alike. This harmonious blend promises an enriching reading experience that celebrates the legacy of traditional storytelling while pushing boundaries to chart new territories in the realm of fantasy fiction.

As we wrap up this opening exploration into the magical and tumultuous world where classic fantasy dances with innovative mythology, we must recognize how these elements are not just thrown together haphazardly. Instead, they are woven with a deft touch, ensuring that each thread—whether age-old or freshly spun—adds strength and vibrancy to the overall tapestry of the tale.

This meticulous integration caters to those who have a deep love for traditional narratives while paving the way for newcomers eager for a taste of originality in their fantastical journeys.

Reflecting on the classics, we see characters like Merlin and Morganna not merely as they were but rejuvenated, placed in scenarios that test their old wisdom against new challenges. This resurgence of familiar faces in unfamiliar situations does more than nod to the past; it breathes new life into it, making every turn of the page both a reunion and a discovery.

Introducing **new mythical creatures is crucial** in keeping the narrative fresh and engaging. These beings bring with them not just intrigue but also a new set of dynamics that interact with the established lore, encouraging readers to rethink what they know about the world and its magical laws. This isn't just a story being told—it's a world being built, piece by piece, creature by creature.

The true magic lies in the balance—the delicate act of merging the known's comfort with the new's thrill. By doing so, the story doesn't just cater to one audience. Still, it opens its arms wide to embrace all lovers of fantasy, whether they've walked these paths before or are just strapping on their boots. This approach not only broadens the appeal of the narrative but also deepens it, allowing for a richer, more immersive experience.

Looking ahead, what awaits is a journey that promises to be as enriching as it is exciting. Each chapter that follows will build on this foundation, exploring deeper into the complexities of character and magic and the nuances of conflict and power. For anyone with a heart for adventure and a curiosity for both the storied past and the uncharted future, this book offers a gateway to experiences that are as thought-provoking as they are thrilling.

Embrace this blend of old and new, familiar and surprising. Let yourself be swept away into a world where magic is not just something you read about but something you feel, deeply and remarkably, as you turn each page. Here's to the journey ahead—may it be as enlightening as it is enchanting.

Chapter 2: Echoes of Universal Strife

Can Power Truly Be Controlled?

Amid the Grand Mage Wars, a young mage named Elara stood in the heart of a decimated village, her boots crunching on charred wood and ashes. The air smelled of smoke and sorrow. She had come here seeking answers, driven by the relentless question that haunted her since she first felt the surge of power within: could anyone truly wield power without succumbing to its intoxicating pull?

Elara's mind wandered back to her mentor, Old Mage Jorin, who once told her that power was like water—necessary for life but devastating in uncontrolled torrents. She remembered his stern face, weathered like the bark of the ancient trees surrounding their sanctuary. *"The challenge,"* he had said, *"is not in gaining power but in channeling it wisely."*

A sudden gust of wind stirred the ashes around her feet into a ghostly dance. Elara watched a small child's toy emerge beneath the gray blanket—a wooden horse with a scorched mane. The sight clenched her heart with grief and strengthened her resolve. She couldn't let this be the end result of power unchecked.

Her thoughts were interrupted by a sharp cry—a lone survivor, an older woman clutching at a tattered shawl, her eyes mirroring the chaos that had swept through her life. Elara approached gently, offering aid with a silent prayer that she might one day mend more than just physical wounds.

As she knelt beside the woman, smoothing back hair as white as winter frost from her wrinkled brow, Elara felt the weight of decisions yet to come. Her choice from here on out could tip the balance towards salvation or ruin.

Could she navigate this treacherous terrain where so many others had faltered? Could anyone?

When Magic Meets Morality: Unraveling the Threads of Power and Ethics

In a world where the arcane arts shape the very fabric of existence, *"The Grand Mage Wars"* offers more than just a thrilling narrative; it mirrors deep philosophical musings on **power, morality**, and conflict resolution. These themes are not just backdrops but are woven intricately into the lives of characters like Merlin and Morganna, challenging readers to question not only the characters' decisions but also their own views on ethics and power.

The Moral Ambiguity of Magic

At its core, this chapter delves into the **complex interplay between good and evil**, a theme as old as time yet forever fresh in its relevance. In its boundless might, magic serves as the perfect metaphor for power—intoxicating and dangerous. Here, we explore how characters grapple with this power, making choices that reveal their complex moral compasses. This exploration is not about casting judgment but understanding the grey spectrum that defines human (and magical) nature.

Bridging Generations through Timeless Themes

The allure of *"The Grand Mage Wars"* stretches across generations—captivating young adults with its vibrant storytelling and engaging older readers through its thoughtful examination of age-old dilemmas. This chapter highlights how themes like **sacrifice, betrayal,** and redemption resonate differently with various age groups, each bringing their unique perspectives and life experiences to their interpretation of the narrative.

FOSTERING COMMUNITY Through Discussion

A significant aspect of this chapter is its focus on the role of these universal themes in sparking dialogues among readers. Whether it's online forums, book clubs, or casual conversations, discussions about the moral implications of Merlin's strategies or Morganna's ambitions encourage a deeper engagement with the text. Such discussions often extend beyond the book's pages, prompting readers to confront similar issues in their own lives.

The narrative's richness lies in its ability to pose questions without easy answers. It invites readers to debate, discuss, and reflect—activities that deepen one's understanding of the text and foster community among readers from diverse backgrounds. Through this shared journey into the world of magic and myth, readers find common ground in their quest for meaning and truth.

In this chapter, we set the stage for these explorations. We sketch out how *"The Grand Mage Wars"* does more than entertain; it provokes thought and invites a reflective examination of our world's ethical dilemmas mirrored through magical conflicts. As we peel back layers of each character's actions and motivations, we look into a mirror, questioning how we, too, might wield power in our lives.

THE GRAND MAGE WARS: THE BATTLE OF LEGENDS UNFOLD

Thus begins our journey into *Echoes of Universal Strife*—a journey that promises to be as enlightening as it is enthralling. With each page turned, we delve deeper into ancient conflicts where magic meets myth, discovering that every spell cast is not just an act of power but also a profound statement on morality.

In *"The Grand Mage Wars,"* the exploration of universal themes such as moral ambiguity and power takes center stage, captivating readers with its intricate complexities. The narrative delves into the shades of gray that define morality, showcasing characters faced with challenging decisions where right and wrong blur into a nebulous realm. This nuanced approach adds layers to the storytelling, inviting readers to ponder the intricacies of human nature and ethical dilemmas.

Within the story's tapestry, power emerges as a driving force, shaping destinies and sparking conflicts reverberating through the ages. Characters grapple with the seductive allure of power, navigating its treacherous waters while striving to maintain their integrity. The exploration of power dynamics serves as a mirror reflecting the ambitions and vulnerabilities within each individual, resonating with readers on a profound level.

As the narrative unfolds, readers are drawn into a world where choices carry weight and consequences ripple across time and space. The themes of moral ambiguity and power intertwine, creating a rich tapestry of human experiences that transcend the boundaries of fantasy. Readers are invited to confront their beliefs and values through the characters' struggles and triumphs, prompting introspection and contemplation.

The allure of these universal themes lies in their ability to transcend age barriers, appealing to both younger audiences seeking adventure and older readers craving depth and complexity. **By weaving moral dilemmas and power struggles into the fabric of the narrative, "The**

Grand Mage Wars" offers something for **everyone,** from those seeking thrilling escapades to individuals yearning for thought-provoking reflections on life's complexities.

Through the characters' journeys, readers are encouraged to explore their relationships with power and morality, inviting introspection and self-discovery. The narrative serves as a mirror reflecting the multifaceted nature of humanity, challenging readers to confront their biases and preconceptions in a world where nothing is black or white.

Embark on this enchanting tale that delves deep into the heart of moral ambiguity and power dynamics. It invites you to ponder your own beliefs and values in a world where choices shape destinies.

Resonance Across Generations

The moral ambiguity and power themes within *"The Grand Mage Wars"* resonate deeply across different age groups, offering a multifaceted appeal that transcends generational boundaries.

Younger readers are drawn to the complexities of morality portrayed in the characters' decisions, often grappling with shades of grey in a world that can seem black and white. The exploration of power dynamics and its consequences mirrors their experiences navigating authority figures and peer relationships, resonating with the challenges they face in finding their place in the world.

For older readers, these themes evoke a sense of nostalgia for the struggles and triumphs they encountered in their youth. The moral dilemmas presented in the narrative trigger reflections on past decisions and the consequences of wielding power, inviting contemplation on personal growth and redemption. The interplay between characters, as they navigate intricate power structures, mirrors the complexities of adult relationships and societal hierarchies, striking a chord with those who have experienced life's many twists and turns.

Middle-aged readers caught between the idealism of youth and the wisdom of experience find themselves at a crossroads where moral ambiguity and power dynamics intersect. The narrative offers them a fresh perspective on these universal themes, reigniting a sense of wonder and introspection as they delve into a world where magic meets myth. The struggles in the story resonate with their journey of self-discovery, prompting them to reevaluate their values and beliefs in light of new revelations.

The themes of moral ambiguity and power serve as a common thread that binds readers together in their exploration of human nature across all age groups. The diverse perspectives presented in the narrative encourage empathy and understanding, fostering meaningful discussions that transcend generational divides. As readers engage with characters facing moral dilemmas and power struggles, they are prompted to reflect on their experiences and beliefs, creating a shared space for introspection and growth.

The timeless nature of these themes ensures readers from different age groups can find relevance and resonance in "The Grand Mage Wars," forging connections that span generations. By delving into the complexities of morality and power, readers are invited to embark on self-discovery and contemplation, uncovering truths about themselves and the world around them.

Broadening Perspectives through Dialogue

Engaging in community discussions surrounding universal themes like moral ambiguity and power can enrich our understanding of complex issues. By sharing diverse viewpoints and personal reflections, readers can gain new insights and perspectives that challenge their preconceived notions. *Encouraging open dialogue* fosters a sense of empathy and understanding, allowing individuals to see beyond their own experiences and consider alternative viewpoints.

Empowering Readers through Engagement

Through active participation in community discussions, readers can voice their opinions, ask questions, and engage in meaningful conversations with others. This engagement deepens their connection to the narrative. It empowers them to explore their beliefs and values in a supportive environment. *By actively participating,* readers can shape the direction of the conversation and contribute to a more inclusive and diverse community.

Inspiring Change Through Reflection

Reflecting on the implications of universal themes within the narrative can inspire readers to enact positive change in their lives and communities. By examining how characters navigate moral dilemmas or wield power, readers can draw parallels to real-world situations and consider how they might approach similar challenges. *Encouraging introspection* can lead to personal growth and a greater sense of agency in shaping one's narrative.

Building a Supportive Community

Community discussions centered around universal themes create a space for readers to connect with like-minded individuals who share a passion for storytelling and exploration. This sense of camaraderie fosters a supportive environment where individuals can express themselves freely, share their interpretations of the narrative, and seek guidance from others. *Creating a sense of belonging* within the community enhances reader engagement and encourages ongoing participation.

Facilitating Meaningful Connections

By delving into the complexities of moral ambiguity and power dynamics in the narrative, readers can form meaningful connections with the story and fellow community members. These connections transcend boundaries of age or background, uniting individuals through shared experiences and common interests.

Fostering connections within the community cultivates a sense of belonging and encourages continued exploration of universal themes.

Encouraging Critical Thinking

Engaging with universal themes in community discussions challenges readers to think critically about complex issues and consider multiple perspectives before forming conclusions. By promoting intellectual curiosity and analytical thinking, these discussions encourage readers to question assumptions, evaluate evidence, and develop well-rounded opinions. *Urging critical reflection* enhances reader engagement by encouraging active participation in thought-provoking conversations.

Cultivating Empathy and Understanding

Through dialogue that explores universal themes such as moral ambiguity and power dynamics, readers can cultivate empathy toward characters facing difficult decisions or navigating intricate power structures. This empathetic connection extends beyond the pages of the narrative, encouraging readers to empathize with others in their own lives who may be grappling with similar challenges. *Promoting empathy* fosters a deeper appreciation for diverse perspectives and encourages compassionate interactions within the community.

Engaging in community discussions that delve into universal themes allows readers to connect with others, reflect on their beliefs, and broaden their perspectives. By fostering an inclusive environment that values diverse viewpoints and encourages critical thinking, readers can deepen their engagement with the narrative while cultivating empathy, understanding, and personal growth.

Exploring universal themes is not just an academic exercise; it's a journey into the heart of being human. By delving into the moral ambiguities and power struggles depicted in our story, readers of all ages find a mirror reflecting their personal and societal conflicts.

This reflection does not merely exist for contemplation. Still, it prompts active engagement and discussion, enriching our understanding of the narrative and ourselves.

Step 1: Identify the universal themes. Start by engaging deeply with the text, noting how the characters navigate the treacherous waters of power dynamics and ethical dilemmas. This initial step is crucial as it sets the stage for all subsequent analysis and discussion.

Step 2: Examine the resonance of these themes. Consider the impact these themes have across various age groups. Younger readers might grapple with these ideas for the first time. At the same time, older audiences might reflect on past experiences, viewing the themes through the lens of wisdom gained over the years.

Step 3: Discuss the implications of these themes. Participation in discussions, whether in book clubs or online forums, opens up new perspectives and deepens the dialogue around the themes. This interaction is vital to enhancing collective understanding and appreciation of the narrative's complexity.

Step 4: Reflect on personal experiences. Connecting the story's themes to one's life experiences can be profoundly transformative. It allows for a personal stake in the themes, making the narrative more relevant and impactful.

Step 5: Share insights and perspectives. Sharing your thoughts and analyses with others broadens your perspective. It helps build a community of thoughtful, engaged readers who enrich each other's understanding of the text.

Step 6: Apply the themes to other narratives. Drawing parallels between this story and other works of literature or real-world events can illuminate new insights and foster a greater appreciation of literary analysis and its relevance to everyday life.

Step 7: Take action. Finally, let these insights inspire personal growth and change. The themes explored motivate readers to evaluate their values and actions, encouraging them to grow and perhaps even to inspire others in their community.

Through this structured exploration, we not only engage with a rich tapestry of narrative elements but also equip ourselves with a deeper understanding that transcends the pages of any book. This exploration fosters a robust dialogue that bridges generational divides, encouraging a shared journey that is as reflective as communal. By reflecting on these themes, sharing our insights, and applying them to other contexts, we continue a tradition of ancient and eternally new storytelling—a testament to the enduring power of literature to shape, reflect, and challenge the human experience.

Chapter 3: Depths of Character

Can One Truly Understand the Heart of Another?

In the quiet village of Eldoria, nestled between whispering woods and serene hills, lived Eleanor, a young scribe whose passion for ancient tales rivaled the age of the stones that paved her narrow streets. Today, like any other, she found herself in the local library—a quaint, ivy-clad building that smelled of old books and adventure. Her fingers brushed against the spines of countless volumes, each a gateway to another world.

Eleanor paused by a shelf that cradled dusty tomes about legendary figures. Her eyes settled on a book titled *"The Grand Mage Wars,"* its cover worn from years of eager readers delving into its depths.

As she flipped through its pages, she was drawn not just by the magic and conflict but by the characters—Merlin and Morganna—whose lives were inked across the parchment. They were not mere magicians but complex souls with fears and dreams as vivid as hers.

Outside, the wind carried laughter from children playing in the market square. Still, Eleanor's mind echoed thoughts deeper than any child's game. She pondered Merlin's struggle with his destiny and Morganna's fierce desire to forge her path despite societal constraints. These characters transcended their mythical roles; they grappled with issues of power, freedom, and what it meant to be misunderstood by those around them.

As she read about Merlin's silent battles with his inner demons and Morganna's external defiance against those who doubted her worth, Eleanor felt a kinship form—a bridge built not just on awe for their magical abilities but on an emotional connection fostered through their humanly flawed experiences. This connection was interrupted by a sudden gust that sent papers flying off a nearby desk, snapping Eleanor back to reality.

She gathered the scattered sheets, each touch to paper reminding her that these characters' journeys were mirrors reflecting her own doubts and victories in life's relentless battles. Why did these stories resonate so deeply within her? Was it their mystical allure or something more profound?

As nightfall approached and shadows danced along the library walls cast by flickering candles, Eleanor knew that understanding oneself through others' stories was perhaps one of life's most intricate spells.

Are we all not looking for pieces of ourselves in others' tales?

Unveiling the Souls Behind the Spells

At the heart of any memorable tale are characters that breathe, bleed, and beguile. *"The Grand Mage Wars"* excels in its grandeur of magical confrontations and, more profoundly, through its in-depth exploration of Merlin and Morganna. These are not merely characters; they are vivid personalities with rich pasts, compelling philosophical stances, and transformative journeys. As we delve into this chapter, we're set to unravel the complex tapestry of their lives, giving us a lens to view their actions and very souls.

The Significance of Backstories

Understanding where someone comes from is pivotal in understanding why they act the way they do. Merlin and Morganna's backstories are not just filler content but essential narratives that shape their present and future decisions. Analyzing these histories shows the foundation of their conflicts and alliances. This chapter promises a journey into their pasts—exploring events that molded Merlin's wisdom and the shadows that haunt Morganna.

Emotional Journeys and Philosophical Beliefs

Emotions drive actions. This chapter will explore how Merlin's philosophies on power and responsibility influence his decisions during crises. Similarly, we will examine Morganna's emotional turmoil and her philosophical evolution from vengeance to redemption. These journeys are not linear; they are fraught with challenges that push them towards growth or despair, making them relatable and real.

Enhancing Narrative Engagement Through Character Depth

The depth of a character does more than enrich a story—it transforms it. It allows readers to connect emotionally with Merlin and Morganna, cheering for their victories and empathizing with their defeats. This chapter highlights how their complexities enhance our engagement with the narrative, turning passive reading into an emotionally active experience.

In weaving these elements together, this exploration does not merely recount events but invites us into the minds and hearts of these legendary figures. Through their stories, we witness the power of deep character development in crafting a story that resonates well beyond its final pages.

By embedding genuine human struggles within a fantastical context, the narrative bridges the gap between myth and reality.

This approach allows readers to reflect on their own life philosophies and emotional journeys through the mirrored experiences of Merlin and Morganna.

Engagement through empathy—this is what turns a good story into a great saga. As we venture deeper into their worlds, we uncover layers that challenge our perceptions and engage our emotions. This isn't just about observing battles between mages but understanding the fighting within themselves.

This chapter sets the stage for a profound exploration of what it means to be heroic in the face of overwhelming odds—not just through magical prowess but through inner strength and moral conviction. Join us as we peel back the layers of enchantment to reveal the human core at the heart of *"The Grand Mage Wars."*

Merlin and Morganna, the central figures in this fantastical tale, are not mere characters but intricate beings with rich backstories that shape their present actions and future destinies. ***Merlin***, the wise and enigmatic wizard, carries the weight of centuries of knowledge and experience within him. Born of humble beginnings, his journey from a young prodigy to the revered Grand Mage is a testament to his resilience and unwavering dedication to mastering the arcane arts. His past is a tapestry woven with threads of triumphs and failures, each contributing to the complex persona he embodies today.

On the other hand, Morganna is a character shrouded in mystery and darkness. Her origins trace back to a lineage of powerful sorcerers tainted by ambition and betrayal. Raised in a world where treachery lurked around every corner, Morganna's path toward embracing her magical gifts was fraught with challenges that tested her resolve and morality. Her backstory unveils layers of vulnerability and strength, painting a portrait of a woman caught between her desires for power and her inner struggle for redemption.

As we delve deeper into their pasts, we uncover the foundations upon which their present choices are built. *The complexities of Merlin and Morganna's histories add depth and nuance to their characters*, allowing readers to empathize with their dilemmas and root for their evolution throughout the narrative. We understand why they act as they do now by understanding where they come from.

EMBRACE THE JOURNEY into Merlin and Morganna's pasts to unravel the mysteries that shape their destinies.

In exploring Merlin and Morganna's emotional journeys and philosophical beliefs, we uncover a tapestry of complexity that adds depth to their characters. **With** his unwavering dedication to preserving the balance of magic in the world, Merlin carries the weight of centuries on his shoulders. His journey is self-discovery, grappling with the consequences of power and the sacrifices it demands. **On** the other hand, Morganna embodies a different kind of struggle, torn between her desire for power and her inner conflict about the ethical use of magic.

Merlin's philosophical beliefs are rooted in a deep respect for the natural order of things. His wisdom comes from age and experience, shaping his understanding of magic as a force that must be wielded responsibly. His emotional journey is one of resilience, facing challenges that test his resolve and integrity. **On** the contrary,

Morganna represents a character driven by ambition and a thirst for power. Her philosophical beliefs are shrouded in shadows, reflecting a more pragmatic approach to magic that blurs the lines between right and wrong.

As we delve into their emotional landscapes, we witness the vulnerability and strength that humanize these legendary figures. *Merlin's* struggles with self-doubt and guilt reveal a relatable aspect of his character, making him more than just a mythical figure but a flawed individual striving to do what is right.

Morganna's internal conflicts expose her inner turmoil, showcasing the complexity of her motivations and desires.

Their journeys are about external battles and internal wars waged within their hearts and minds. *Merlin* grapples with the burden of his past choices, seeking redemption through selflessness and bravery. *On* the other hand, Morganna faces a constant battle between her ambitions and her conscience, torn between what she wants and what she knows is right.

Through their emotional journeys and philosophical beliefs, *Merlin and Morganna* become more than characters in a story; they embody universal themes of sacrifice, redemption, power, and morality. Their evolution throughout the narrative mirrors our struggles and triumphs, inviting us to reflect on our choices and beliefs.

In unraveling the layers of their characters, we are reminded that proper depth lies not in perfection but imperfection. Through their flaws and vulnerabilities, *Merlin and Morganna* resonate with us on a profound level, sparking introspection and empathy within ourselves. Their emotional journeys serve as beacons of light in the darkness, guiding us to confront our shadows and embrace our humanity.

THE GRAND MAGE WARS: THE BATTLE OF LEGENDS UNFOLD

As we witness their transformations unfold, we are compelled to question our own paths - what sacrifices are we willing to make for our beliefs? How do we navigate the murky waters of morality in a world filled with shades of gray? ***Merlin's*** unwavering faith in goodness and ***Morganna's*** relentless pursuit of power challenge us to confront our values and principles, urging us to embark on our quests for truth and meaning.

Reflecting on the depths of character within *"The Grand Mage Wars"* reveals how **character depth enhances emotional engagement** with the narrative. As readers delve into the intricate personas of **Merlin and Morganna**, they find themselves drawn into a world where philosophical beliefs, personal histories, and evolving journeys intertwine to create a tapestry of relatable struggles and triumphs. This emotional connection transcends mere observation, allowing readers to invest in the characters' lives and outcomes on a profound level.

Through Merlin and Morganna's complex backstories, readers witness the shaping of their identities and understand the motivations behind their actions and beliefs. These detailed histories provide a rich foundation for the characters, offering insights into their past traumas, joys, and formative experiences.

By unraveling the layers of their pasts, readers are invited to empathize with their struggles and celebrate their victories, forging a bond that transcends the book's pages.

Exploring Merlin and Morganna's emotional journeys further deepens the reader's engagement with the narrative. As these characters grapple with internal conflicts, moral dilemmas, and personal growth, readers are invited to reflect on their journeys of self-discovery and transformation. The emotional resonance of these experiences resonates with readers on a visceral level, fostering a sense of connection and shared humanity that transcends differences in time or space.

Moreover, delving into the ***philosophical beliefs that*** guide Merlin and Morganna's actions adds another layer of depth to their characters. By examining their worldviews, values, and ethical codes, readers are prompted to ponder universal truths about morality, power, destiny, and free will. This exploration enriches the narrative and challenges readers to reflect on their beliefs and principles, sparking introspection and growth in unexpected ways.

In essence, ***character depth*** is a gateway to enhanced emotional engagement with the narrative of *"The Grand Mage Wars."* By immersing readers in the complexities of Merlin and Morganna's personas, this depth invites them to connect on a deeper level with the characters' joys, sorrows, hopes, and fears. Through this emotional resonance, readers are not merely spectators but active participants in the unfolding tale of magic and myth, forging bonds that transcend fiction to touch upon universal truths about love, loss, redemption, and the enduring power of human connection.

As readers navigate the intricacies of Merlin and Morganna's characters, they are encouraged to embrace empathy, introspection, and open-mindedness in their own lives. The journey through the depths of character in *"The Grand Mage Wars"* serves as a mirror reflecting back our own complexities and contradictions. It prompts us to confront our shadows, embrace our light, and embark on our quests for self-discovery and growth. In this shared exploration of humanity's timeless struggles and triumphs lies the true magic of storytelling—the ability to transform hearts and minds through the power of empathetic connection.

In exploring the intricacies of Merlin and Morganna's characters, we've delved deep into their backstories, emotional journeys, and philosophical beliefs. This exploration is not merely academic; it serves a vital role in drawing us closer to these legendary figures, making their conflicts and triumphs our own. By understanding their complexities, we foster a connection that elevates our experience from simply reading about magical battles to feeling deeply invested in the outcomes of these characters.

The importance of character depth must be balanced. This depth transforms our reading experience, allowing us to see parts of ourselves reflected in these characters. Whether Merlin's wise yet often troubled demeanor or Morganna's fierce independence is shadowed by her inner conflicts, we find elements that resonate personally. This connection is crucial; it turns the narrative from a distant myth into a mirror reflecting our world and struggles.

Throughout this chapter, we've seen how characters' emotional and philosophical growth enriches a story. It's one thing to read about Merlin's strategic maneuvers or Morganna's powerful sorcery; it's another to understand why they take these actions. What drives Merlin's dedication to protecting his realm? What fears and ambitions push Morganna to her limits? These questions give substance to their magic, grounding their fantastical elements in human reality.

Moreover, engaging with these characters on multiple levels encourages us to reflect on our beliefs and experiences. We navigate our philosophical and emotional landscapes as we align our feelings with Merlin's dilemmas or Morganna's challenges.

This introspection is a powerful aspect of reading, one that enriches not only our understanding of the text but also of ourselves.

Lastly, let us remember that the stories we cherish most often speak directly to our hearts, making us feel seen and understood. The narrative invites us into a more profound engagement by presenting characters like Merlin and Morganna not just as figures of power but as beings with deeply woven tales and emotional complexities. It encourages us to explore, question, and even learn from the journey alongside them.

As we close this chapter, let's carry forward the understanding that the strength of a tale lies not just in its plot or its magical spectacle but profoundly in its ability to weave complex characters whose journeys inspire, challenge, and transform us. This is what makes a story readable and relivable—time and again.

Chapter 4: Arcane Realms of Reason

The Weight of Authenticity in a World of Magic

In the early hours of a brisk spring morning, just as the sun cast pale hues over the horizon, Marlow found himself pacing the length of his small, cluttered study. Books lay strewn about, pages filled with arcane symbols and ancient lore flapping like captured birds wanting to take flight. He paused by the window, watching a lone sparrow peck at the fresh blooms in his garden. The simplicity of its existence taunted him, contrasting sharply with the complexity of his own.

Marlow was no ordinary man; he was a mage in a world where magic was as real as the ground underfoot and just as treacherous. He had recently uncovered discrepancies in *"The Grand Mage Wars,"* an old text that served as a historical document and instructional tome for young mages. His discovery suggested that magic could be more structured and authentic than previously believed. This revelation could transform their understanding and application of magical forces, aligning them closer to nature's inherent laws rather than mere chaotic bursts of power.

He returned to his desk, fingers tracing the lines of an open book. The scent of musty paper filled his nostrils as he absorbed words that seemed to dance and shift before his eyes. His mind wandered back to his early days at the academy, where old Professor Lyndon insisted that magic was a living thing; it evolved just like creatures of flesh and blood. Marlow had scoffed then but suspected Lyndon might have been onto something profound.

A knock on the door jolted him from his thoughts. It was Clara, his apprentice, her eyes bright with curiosity and something akin to concern.

"Master Marlow," she began hesitantly, *"the council summons you. They've heard rumors about your... theories."*

Marlow nodded slowly, understanding all too well what this meant. The council feared change and clung to old beliefs like a shipwrecked sailor to flotsam. As he followed Clara into the chill morning air that whipped their cloaks around fiercely like flags in a storm, Marlow felt an old fire rekindle within him—a mixture of defiance and excitement.

Would this new understanding lead them to enlightenment or plunge them deeper into chaos?

Unveiling the Logic Behind the Magic

Magic in fantasy literature often feels like it emerges from the murky depths of the inexplicable, with rules as shifting and elusive as shadows at dusk. However, in *"The Grand Mage Wars: The Battle of Legends Unfold,"* we encounter a refreshing deviation that enchants and makes eminent sense. This chapter delves into the structured magical systems that are as integral to the storyline as they are reflective of our characters' journeys and the thematic depth of the narrative.

The Foundation of Magical Realism

At first glance, the magic in our tale might seem to defy logic, a whimsical counterpart to the harsh realities of Merlin and Morganna's world. Yet, upon closer inspection, it is clear that these magical systems are painstakingly crafted with rules that ensure consistency and believability. Here, we see magic not as a mere tool for convenience or an arbitrary element used to resolve unsolvable conflicts but as a well-thought-out mechanism that propels the plot forward and deepens our understanding of the characters.

Reflecting Character Growth Through Magic

Each spell cast and mystical barrier confronted is a mirror reflecting our protagonists' personal growth and evolving philosophies. As readers, we witness how challenges within these arcane realms shape character development and thematic resonance throughout the story. The magic system does not just exist; it evolves, adapts, and responds to the shifting landscapes of our characters' internal and external worlds.

Thematic Echoes in Magical Laws

The logic of magic within this narrative serves a dual purpose—it is practical and profoundly thematic. As characters wrestle with their powers, they grapple with more prominent existential themes of power, responsibility, and transformation. These themes are intricately woven into how magic operates in this universe, making every magical act a thematic exploration as much as a plot-driving force.

Realism in Fantasy: A Paradox?

Introducing realism into a fantasy context might seem contradictory at first. Yet, precisely, this blend of the fantastical with the logical anchors our story in a relatable reality. Readers believe in the magic because its application follows discernible rules and consequences that mirror real-world cause and effect. This realism invites readers deeper into the narrative, encouraging them to invest more fully in the characters' struggles and triumphs.

The Crucial Role of Consistency

Consistency in how magical elements are portrayed ensures that once readers suspend their disbelief, they are rewarded with a story that remains internally coherent. This consistency builds trust between reader and writer, allowing for deeper immersion into the complexities of the plot without fear of unexpected breaks in narrative logic.

In exploring these facets—***the structured magical* systems**, their reflection in ***character evolution***, and their role in enhancing ***narrative realism***—we uncover how magic works in *"The Grand Mage Wars"* and why it matters. The magic here is more than spectacle; it is substance. It carries weight and consequences, shaping destinies while reflecting deeper truths about our world.

As we progress through this exploration, let us appreciate how meticulously crafted details can transform seemingly whimsical elements into pivotal storytelling that engages our imagination and intellect.

Magic in *"The Grand Mage Wars"* is not a chaotic force but a structured system with rules and limitations that add depth and authenticity to the narrative. Within this world, magic is not a whimsical tool used arbitrarily but a well-defined force that characters must understand and master. The magical systems in the plot are meticulously crafted to serve a purpose beyond mere spectacle; they mirror the character growth and thematic undercurrents of the story, enriching the reader's experience.

In this fantastical realm, magic is not just about flashy spells or enchantments but about logic and reason. Each magical element introduced in the story has a specific function and follows principles that govern its use. This structured approach adds a layer of realism to the fantastical elements, making them more believable and integral to the plot's progression. ***By grounding magic in rules and limitations, the narrative creates a sense of consistency and coherence, enhancing the storytelling.***

THE GRAND MAGE WARS: THE BATTLE OF LEGENDS UNFOLD

The magical systems explored in *"The Grand Mage Wars"* are not static but evolve alongside the characters, reflecting their growth and transformation throughout the narrative. As protagonists learn new spells or delve deeper into ancient magical practices, their journey parallels their personal development, adding depth to their arcs. ***This interplay between magic and character evolution creates a rich tapestry of interconnected themes and motifs*** that resonate with readers profoundly.

Furthermore, these magical systems are not isolated entities within the story but are intricately woven into the fabric of the world-building. ***They shape societies, influence power dynamics, and drive conflicts***, highlighting the significance of magic as more than just a plot device. By exploring the nuances of these magical systems, readers gain insight into the intricate web of relationships that define this fantastical realm.

Delving into the structured magical systems used in *"The Grand Mage Wars"* is akin to unraveling a complex puzzle where every piece fits together with purpose and precision. ***Each spell, ritual, or enchantment serves a specific function within the narrative***, contributing to the overarching themes and character arcs. By understanding these magical systems, readers can appreciate the meticulous craftsmanship behind the fantastical elements in the story.

Continue reading to discover how these magical systems reflect the characters' evolution and thematic undercurrents in "The Grand Mage Wars."

In *"The Grand Mage Wars,"* the magical systems are not just tools for characters to wield; they are mirrors reflecting their evolution and the underlying themes of the narrative. Each character's journey is intricately woven with the magic they possess, shaping their growth and contributing to the thematic richness of the story.

Magic is not merely a spectacle but a profound element that intertwines with the character's development and the overarching messages of the tale.

As characters navigate challenges and conflicts, their magical abilities transform with their personal growth. *The evolution of magic in the story parallels the inner transformations of the characters,* serving as a visual representation of their struggles, triumphs, and evolving understanding of themselves and the world around them. The authenticity of these magical evolutions adds depth to the characters, making them more relatable and multi-dimensional.

Thematic undercurrents run deep within the magical systems, resonating with broader ideas and messages woven into the narrative. Readers can decipher metaphors, symbolism, and allegories that enrich the storytelling experience through these systems. *Magic becomes a vehicle for exploring complex themes such as power, destiny, sacrifice, and redemption* tangibly and engagingly.

The narrative achieves a harmonious balance between spectacle and substance by aligning magical systems with character arcs and thematic undercurrents. The magic in *"The Grand Mage Wars"* serves a dual purpose: it dazzles with its fantastical elements while grounding the story in emotional depth and philosophical contemplation. This fusion creates a cohesive narrative where magic is not just a plot device but an integral part of character development and thematic exploration.

Through the reflection of characters' evolution in magical systems, readers are invited to introspect on their own growth journeys. The parallel between magical transformations and personal development encourages readers to consider how their experiences shape them over time. By immersing themselves in these interconnected narratives of magic and self-discovery, readers may find inspiration to embrace change, confront challenges, and embark on their growth paths.

In *"The Grand Mage Wars,"* **magic is not static but dynamic**, mirroring the fluid nature of life itself. As characters adapt and evolve, so does their magic, reflecting the ever-changing landscape of their inner worlds. This fluidity encourages readers to embrace change as an essential part of growth and transformation, inspiring them to navigate life's twists and turns with resilience and adaptability.

Ultimately, by intertwining magical systems with character evolution and thematic undercurrents, "The Grand Mage Wars" profoundly elevates its storytelling. Magic becomes more than just spells and enchantments; it reflects human experiences—of growth, struggle, triumph, and self-discovery. In this intricate tapestry of magic and meaning, readers find entertainment and profound insights into the complexities of existence.

Descriptive Framework: Magical Systems Analysis

A structured framework is essential for analyzing the magical systems within the narrative and grasping the depth and evolution of magic in *"The Grand Mage Wars."* This framework delves into the core principles, character interactions, comparative analysis, and critical reflections that shape the authenticity and consistency of the magical elements in the story.

Core Principles of Magic

The magical universe in the narrative is rooted in well-defined principles that govern the source, limitations, and utilization of magic. **Magic derives from ancient ley lines** that weave through the world, providing a tangible connection to mystical energies. **Limitations** are crucial, ensuring magic does not become an all-solving force but rather a nuanced tool with consequences. **Accessing magic** involves intricate rituals, incantations, or innate abilities possessed by characters, setting a clear foundation for how magic operates.

Evolution of Magical Systems

As characters navigate their arcs, their growth intertwines with shifts in magical abilities. **Key moments** mark pivotal changes where characters gain new powers or face challenges restricting their magical prowess. These developments mirror the narrative's personal growth and thematic elements, showcasing a parallel evolution between characters and magic.

Comparative Analysis

Comparing *"The Grand Mage Wars"* magical systems with classic and contemporary fantasy literature unveils the innovation and uniqueness of this narrative. **Distinctive elements** such as interconnected ley lines, consequences for magic usage, and personalized spells set it apart from traditional portrayals of magic. This analysis highlights how the story contributes to the genre by reimagining magical conventions with depth and purpose.

Critical Reflections

Encouraging readers to delve deeper into the realism and consistency of magical elements prompts introspection on how these aspects enhance believability. **Questions** like how well magic aligns with character development or thematic motifs spark critical engagement with the narrative's world-building. By fostering discussions on coherence and authenticity, readers can appreciate the meticulous crafting of magic within *"The Grand Mage Wars."*

This framework provides a comprehensive lens through which readers can explore and appreciate the intricate tapestry of magical systems

THE GRAND MAGE WARS: THE BATTLE OF LEGENDS UNFOLD

in the narrative. Dissecting core principles, character evolution, comparative analysis, and critical reflections reveal a deeper understanding of magic's role in shaping characters and the storyline.

As we wrap up our exploration of the arcane realms within the narrative, it's clear that the magical systems employed are not just tools for fantastical battles but are intricately woven into the very fabric of character development and thematic depth. This seamless integration ensures that each spell cast and arcane discovery is exciting and deeply meaningful.

Step 1: Identify the different magical systems. These systems offer a lens through which to view the complexity and creativity of the author's world. By understanding the rules and limitations, readers can appreciate the characters' challenges and triumphs.

Moving to ***Step 2: Examine the connection between magical systems and characters' evolution***; we see magic as a catalyst for personal growth. The journey through mastering these powers parallels the characters' internal battles and victories, reflecting their evolving identities and ambitions.

Step 3: Evaluate the consistency and realism of magical elements. This step forces us to consider how grounded these systems are within the story's universe. Consistency in these rules makes the unbelievable believable, allowing us to suspend disbelief and immerse ourselves fully in the narrative.

Step 4: Compare and contrast magical systems to encourage a broader perspective, positioning our story within the more significant fantasy genre. This comparison highlights what is unique about our tale. It enhances our appreciation for how magical systems can vary widely yet serve similar narrative purposes.

In ***Step 5: Discuss the thematic implications of magical systems***, we delve into the deeper meanings behind magical prowess. Power dynamics, ethical dilemmas, and the struggle between good and evil are refracted through the prism of magic, offering a rich ground for philosophical exploration.

Step 6: Critical analysis challenges us to not just passively consume but also actively engage with the material. We dialogue with the text by questioning and critiquing, contributing to a deeper understanding and appreciation of its complexities.

Finally, ***Step 7: Share your findings*** reminds us that stories are meant to be shared. Discussions and debates about the magic systems can enhance our enjoyment and understanding of the book while connecting us with a community of fellow readers.

Each step here is designed to analyze and enrich our reading experience, reminding us that magic in literature is not just about spectacle but about deeper meanings and connections. This structured approach does not confine our imagination. Still, it

expands, allowing us to see beyond the surface and appreciate the subtlety and power of well-crafted magical realms. Through this process, we gain more than just knowledge; we gain a new way to see stories—as mirrors reflecting our world, filled with complexity, beauty, and mystery.

Chapter 5: The Dynamic Reader's Role

Can Imagination Conquer Reality?

A gentle breeze danced through Clara's small, cluttered study curtains in the dim light of early morning. Books lay open on every surface, their pages brimming with tales of ancient wars and grand mages. As the scent of ink and old paper mingled with the fresh air, Clara leaned back in her chair, her mind swirling with images of battles and spells. Today was no ordinary day; she had decided to take up a challenge that had haunted her for years.

Clara's eyes rested on a particular volume titled *"The Grand Mage Wars,"* its cover faded from years of use. She remembered how her grandfather read those stories to her as a child, his voice weaving magic into the air around them. Now, she sought to recreate that magic for others, to make readers feel as alive as she had felt back then.

As she pondered how best to engage her future readers, her cat, Nimbus, jumped onto the table, scattering some papers onto the floor. The sudden disruption pulled Clara from her reverie. She picked up Nimbus and set him gently on her lap, stroking his fur as she returned to her thoughts.

She knew that simply recounting the events would not suffice; she needed to make the stories leap off the page. How could she guide others to see what wasn't there? To not just read but experience?

Her challenge was clear: transform passive reading into an active journey through imagination and critical thought.

Clara envisioned teaching techniques for visualizing scenes vividly and analyzing complex themes deeply. It would be like guiding readers through a labyrinthine garden where every path revealed different fragrances and colors—each turn offering new insights into character motives or hidden story layers.

Outside, a child laughed loudly as he chased another around in a game of tag, their shouts piercing through Clara's concentration momentarily. She smiled briefly before returning focus to her task.

Could these immersive tactics bridge the gap between the reader and the story? Could they truly bring *"The Grand Mage Wars"* alive once more?

Unleashing Your Inner Mage: How to Become Part of the Magic

Imagine stepping into a world where the lines between reader and character blur, where you can almost feel the crackle of magic in the air as ancient conflicts unfold before your eyes. This isn't just about reading; it's about experiencing, engaging, and living within the story. *"The Grand Mage Wars: The Battle of Legends Unfold"* offers more than just words on a page—it invites you to dive deep, think critically, and let your imagination roam free.

Unlocking the Power of Imagination

To truly engage with a narrative like this, one must first learn to harness the power of their own imagination. Every scene in our story is a canvas, and your mind is the brush. Here, we explore how to vividly paint these scenes in your mind's eye, transforming static descriptions into dynamic realities. You're observing and participating as you visualize Merlin's duels or Morganna's enchantments. This chapter will guide you through practical techniques to enhance this visualization process, making each magical encounter more vivid and enthralling.

Critical Reading: Beyond the Surface

However, engaging with a story is not all about imagery; it is also about depth. Critical reading is pivotal in unraveling the complex themes woven through our tale. You see layers of meaning that might otherwise remain hidden by analyzing character motivations, plot twists, and mythical elements. This chapter will equip you with strategies to question and connect deeply with the text. It's about peeling back layers and discovering undercurrents that add richness and texture to your reading experience.

Interactivity: A Two-Way Street

Moreover, interaction with the text doesn't end with visualization and analysis. It also involves making personal connections that resonate with your experiences and emotions. Whether you draw parallels between the legendary battles and personal conflicts or find inspiration in the resilience of our characters, these connections make your journey through *"The Grand Mage Wars"* uniquely rewarding.

Through engaging exercises and thought-provoking questions in this chapter, we encourage you to reflect on how the themes relate to contemporary issues or your life. Such engagement enhances enjoyment and solidifies comprehension and retention of the narrative's key elements.

Engagement is essential, not optional. By actively participating in the unfolding saga, readers transform from passive observers to active co-creators in the storytelling process. This dynamic interaction elevates a good book into a great one—a living experience that extends beyond its pages.

THE GRAND MAGE WARS: THE BATTLE OF LEGENDS UNFOLD 49

As we delve deeper into these tactics throughout this chapter, remember that each strategy is more than just a method; it's an invitation to enter a dialogue with the story and yourself. By employing these tactics, *"The Grand Mage Wars"* becomes more than just a tale to read—it becomes a world to live in, learn from, and love.

In embracing these approaches, you do more than follow a narrative—you breathe life into it. This chapter stands as your guide on this transformative journey, ensuring that each page turned is not just read but felt deeply and remembered fondly.

As you delve into the pages of *"The Grand Mage Wars,"* it's crucial to implement tactics that enhance your reading experience through active imagination. Visualizing the scenes vividly can transport you into the story's heart, immersing yourself fully in the world of Merlin and Morganna. You can breathe life into the narrative by actively engaging your mind and senses, making it a more enriching and captivating journey.

As you read, pay attention to the details when describing settings, characters, and actions. Imagine yourself standing beside Merlin as he conjures spells or feels the chill of Morganna's presence creeping up your spine. ***Visualize the landscapes, hear the whispers of ancient magic, and let your imagination run wild.*** By actively picturing these elements, you enhance your understanding of the story and make it a more personal and intimate experience.

Engage all your senses while reading to create a multi-dimensional experience. Close your eyes and envision the colors of magic swirling around you, feel the texture of ancient tomes beneath your fingertips, and imagine the taste of adventure lingering on your tongue. ***By immersing yourself fully in the sensory details of the narrative, you can make the story come alive in ways that transcend mere words on a page.***

Challenge yourself to go beyond what is explicitly stated in the text. Fill in gaps with your own interpretations, imagine what lies beyond the edges of the map, or ponder the motivations behind each character's actions. *By actively participating in creating the world of "The Grand Mage Wars," you become a co-creator of the story alongside the author.*

Continue reading to discover how critical reading skills can deepen your understanding of complex themes in "The Grand Mage Wars."

Applying critical reading skills is crucial in deepening your understanding of the complex themes woven throughout the narrative. By delving beyond the surface and actively engaging with the text, you can uncover hidden meanings, subtle nuances, and profound messages that enrich your reading experience.

Analyzing character motivations, dissecting plot developments, and questioning underlying assumptions can lead to a more profound connection with the story and its themes.

As you immerse yourself in "The Grand Mage Wars," consider the historical context and cultural references embedded within the narrative. *Researching the inspiration behind certain characters or events can help you* better appreciate the author's craft and intentions. *Drawing parallels between the fictional world and real-life events* can provide valuable insights into universal truths and timeless themes that resonate across different eras.

Challenge yourself to think critically about the choices made by characters, the consequences of their actions, and the moral dilemmas they face. *Consider how these elements reflect broader societal issues* or philosophical questions that invite introspection and self-exploration. *Engaging with the text on multiple levels* allows you to extract layers of meaning and interpret the story through various lenses, enriching your overall reading experience.

Look beyond the surface plot points and explore the underlying themes of power, redemption, sacrifice, or betrayal that shape the narrative landscape. *Identify recurring motifs, symbols, or metaphors* that carry symbolic weight and add depth to the storytelling. *By connecting these literary devices to broader thematic concepts*, you can uncover hidden truths and profound messages that resonate personally and universally.

Embrace ambiguity and complexity, recognizing that not all answers may be clear-cut or definitive. *Allow room for interpretation and multiple perspectives,* acknowledging that different readers may derive varied meanings from the same text.

Engage in discussions with fellow readers, sharing insights, interpretations, and theories to broaden your understanding of the story's intricacies.

You cultivate a deeper appreciation for storytelling craftsmanship and thematic depth by honing your critical reading skills.

Approach each page with curiosity and an open mind, ready to uncover new revelations and insights that enrich your reading journey. *You* enhance your enjoyment of *"The Grand Mage Wars"* through active engagement with complex themes and develop a deeper connection with the characters, settings, and overarching narrative tapestry.

Engaging interactively with the story is crucial to enhancing your enjoyment and comprehension of the narrative. By immersing yourself fully in *"The Grand Mage Wars,"* you can enrich your reading experience and uncover hidden gems within the story.

Take the time to reflect on the characters' motivations, the intricacies of the magical realms, and the underlying themes that shape the narrative. This active participation allows you to connect more deeply with the plot and characters, making the story come alive in your mind.

As you engage interactively with the story, consider adopting a curious mindset. Ask yourself why certain events unfold, ponder the implications of character decisions, and explore the broader impact of the magical elements at play. *By delving into these inquiries, you can better understand the story's nuances and fully appreciate the author's craft.*

Another effective way to enhance your engagement with the narrative is to discuss it with fellow readers. Sharing interpretations, theories, and favorite moments can provide fresh perspectives and insights you might not have considered.

Engaging in discussions about the story can also deepen your emotional connection to the characters and their journeys.

To immerse yourself in "The Grand Mage Wars," consider creating visual aids or mood boards representing vital scenes or characters. This hands-on approach can help solidify your understanding of the story's setting and atmosphere while allowing you to express your creativity tangibly. *Visual representations can also be powerful memory aids, helping you recall essential details as you progress through the narrative.*

Lastly, don't be afraid to let your imagination run wild while engaging with the story. Visualize epic battles, intricate spellcasting, and breathtaking landscapes with vivid detail. Allow yourself to become fully absorbed in "The Grand Mage Wars," letting go of constraints and embracing the fantastical elements with open arms.

THE GRAND MAGE WARS: THE BATTLE OF LEGENDS UNFOLD

By actively engaging with the narrative through reflection, discussion, visual representation, and boundless imagination, you can elevate your reading experience to new heights. ***Embrace these interactive strategies wholeheartedly***, allowing yourself to be swept away by the magic of "The Grand Mage Wars" and all it offers.

As we draw this chapter to a close, it is essential to reflect on the profound impact of active imagination, critical reading, and interactive engagement on your experience of this magical tale. By implementing these strategies, you will enhance your enjoyment and deepen your comprehension of the intricate themes woven throughout the narrative.

Active imagination is a powerful tool, enabling you to visualize the mystical battles and strategic confrontations in vivid detail. This approach makes the scenes more engaging and allows you to connect with the characters deeper, experiencing their dilemmas and triumphs as if they were your own.

Applying *critical reading skills* is equally important. It encourages you to question and analyze the complex themes that underpin the storyline, from the moral ambiguities faced by characters to the broader philosophical questions about power and responsibility.

This critical engagement ensures a richer, more nuanced understanding of the text, which, in turn, enriches your reading experience.

Lastly, *interactive engagement* with the story transforms reading from a passive activity into an active dialogue between you and the text. Whether predicting future plot twists or connecting historical elements with contemporary issues, this interaction fosters a deeper personal connection with the narrative, making each twist and turn all the more impactful.

By embracing these immersive tactics, you play a dynamic role in bringing the enchantment of this ancient conflict to life.

Remember, each page offers an opportunity to explore new realms of imagination and insight. Let your mind wander through the lush landscapes of magic and myth, engage with the characters' complex motivations, and above all, enjoy the journey of discovery at the heart of every book.

The practices discussed here are not just techniques; they are invitations to journey deeper into unknown worlds and truly become part of something larger than oneself. So, as you turn each page, remember that your engagement breathes life into every word, every battle, every moment of victory and defeat. Through your eyes, the legends of Merlin and Morganna are not just revisited—they are revived and reimagined.

May your reading journey be as enchanting and transformative as old tales. Embrace these strategies, dive deep into the heart of this conflict, and let the magic of your imagination set the stage for a truly legendary experience.

Chapter 6: The Unforeseen Magic

Can Magic Ever Be Predictable?

In the small, bustling town of Eldoria, nestled between the whispering woods and the singing river, Jareth, the young mage apprentice, found himself at a crossroads not just of paths but of potential futures. The Grand Mage Wars had begun, with them, a new era where magical laws were no longer constants but variables that evolved like living creatures. Jareth walked through the market square, his mind racing as fast as his heart. The scent of fresh bread from Baker Thom's stall mingled with the earthy aroma of rain that had earlier kissed the cobblestones.

He thought back to his master's words just that morning. *"Magic is changing, boy. What worked yesterday might not work today,"* Master Alric had said, stroking his silver beard, eyes twinkling with excitement and fear. Jareth felt a chill as he remembered those words; they fluttered in his stomach like nervous birds.

Turning a corner, he nearly bumped into Old Mira, the flower seller. Her smile was as warm as the sunflowers she peddled.

"Watch where you're going, young master," she chuckled, her voice a soothing balm to his frazzled nerves. He apologized and paused to help her pick up a few fallen blooms. The simple act grounded him momentarily.

Resuming his walk home under the canopy of twilight stars now blinking into existence above him, Jareth mulled over how unpredictable magic could affect not just duels or wars but daily life itself. How would they heal? How would they build? His footsteps echoed on stone as he passed the closed bookshop and neared the silent library.

The night was cool, and each breath Jareth took seemed to fill him with both dread and wonder about this evolving world of magic.

What did it mean for an apprentice like him? Was there room for error when every spell cast could backfire or fizzle unexpectedly?

As he finally reached his home and pushed open the creaking wooden door, Jareth knew one thing for sure: tomorrow, he would attempt his first spell under these new unpredictable magical laws—a simple light spell to test the waters.

How will magic's unpredictability shape Jareth's future and all who dwell in Eldoria?

Will the Wand Waver or Weave New Wonders?

As we delve deeper into the heart of *"The Grand Mage Wars,"* a striking aspect comes to the forefront—the concept of evolving magical laws. This pivotal narrative device not only stirs the pot of traditional fantasy storytelling but also injects a fresh dose of unpredictability into our reading experience. Imagine a world where magic isn't just a tool but an evolving entity, almost like a character in its own right, capable of changing the rules as the story progresses. This chapter peels back layers of this innovative idea, setting the stage for discussing how such dynamism impacts the story and its audience.

By its very nature, in most fantasy literature, magic is seen as a stable force with established limits and rules. However, in this saga, as we begin to understand more about these evolving magical laws, we witness something extraordinary—*the unpredictability inherent in change*. As these laws transform, so does the strategy and interaction of characters within the tale. It's akin to playing a chess game where the moves and powers of the pieces can change unexpectedly. This element keeps readers on their toes, constantly guessing and reevaluating their expectations.

THE RIPPLE EFFECT OF Unpredictability

When predictability in the plot becomes a thing of the past, each turn of the page increases in anticipation. Readers are not passive observers but active participants trying to discover potential outcomes. This involvement creates a gripping reading experience that challenges our conventional consumption of narrative arcs. It's refreshing, somewhat unsettling, and utterly captivating.

Challenging Conventional Fantasy Tropes

Through various cases highlighted in this narrative arc, we see familiar tropes—like the mentor-apprentice dynamic or the quest for a magical artifact—turned on their heads due to these shifting laws. Characters who might traditionally have specific, predictable paths instead find themselves facing new dilemmas and opportunities that test their mettle in unexpected ways.

This approach revitalizes well-worn paths and encourages readers to question and think critically about the roles and rules often taken for granted in fantasy settings. What happens when the wise old wizard doesn't have all the answers because magic itself is in flux?

How does a hero cope when their trusted magical abilities might alter mid-battle? These questions are not just hypothetical—they're vividly explored through thrilling narrative developments that showcase character growth and plot evolution.

Magic Reinvented: A New Layer of Depth

By introducing evolving magical laws, the story adds a layer of depth to both character development and world-building.

Characters must adapt to these changes—some thriving and others faltering—which mirrors real-life challenges individuals face during change. The unpredictability also serves as a metaphor for life's unpredictable nature, making the fantastical elements resonate more deeply with personal human experiences.

As we journey through this chapter, we expect to explore how an ever-changing magical landscape shapes a narrative and engages us in more profound reflections about adaptability and resilience. The beauty of unpredictability is not just in its ability to surprise but also in its power to inspire and provoke thought beyond conventional boundaries.

As you turn each page filled with unexpected twists dictated by shifting spells and wavering wands, consider how you face changes in your life. Are they obstacles or opportunities? Through this lens, let us traverse this enchanted battleground where legends unfold not only through might and magic but also through adaptability and intellect.

In *"The Grand Mage Wars,"* the concept of evolving magical laws adds a unique and dynamic element to the narrative. Unlike traditional fantasy stories where magic follows rigid, unchanging rules, this tale introduces a sense of unpredictability and growth in the very fabric of its magical system. **The evolving nature of magical laws in the story challenges familiar tropes. It keeps readers engaged by presenting them with unexpected twists and turns.** This innovative approach not only injects freshness into the plot but also encourages readers to think beyond conventional fantasy narratives.

Magic in this world is not static; it evolves, adapts, and surprises both characters and readers. Instead of relying on established norms, the characters must navigate a shifting landscape where magical laws can change in response to actions and events. This unpredictability adds complexity to the story, forcing characters to think creatively and adapt to new challenges as they arise. *By embracing evolving magical laws, "The Grand Mage Wars" breaks away from traditional fantasy storytelling, offering readers a refreshing and immersive experience.*

In this narrative, magic is not a fixed entity governed by set rules; instead, it is fluid and responsive to the unfolding events. *This dynamic nature of magic mirrors the unpredictability of life itself,* where change is constant, and adaptation is vital to survival. By weaving evolving magical laws into the story's fabric, the author invites readers to embrace uncertainty and view it as an opportunity for growth and transformation.

The beauty of evolving magical laws is their ability to surprise and challenge characters and readers. When one thinks they have understood how magic works in this world, a new law or an existing one evolves, reshaping the course of events. This element of surprise keeps the narrative fresh and exciting, compelling readers to stay engaged and eager to unravel what comes next.

Continue reading to delve deeper into how unpredictability affects the story's progression and reader anticipation.

Unpredictability in a story can be powerful, keeping readers engaged and eager to uncover what comes next. In *"The Grand Mage Wars,"* evolving magical laws add a layer of complexity that constantly challenges both the characters within the narrative and the readers themselves. This unpredictability is not random but follows a logical progression based on the changing nature of magic in this fantastical world. ***The story becomes dynamic and fresh by introducing evolving magical laws, steering away from clichés, and offering a unique reading experience.***

As the narrative unfolds, readers are kept on their toes, always trying to figure out what to expect next. This element of surprise injects excitement into the storyline, making each twist and turn all the more thrilling. ***Unpredictability affects the story's progression by creating tension and suspense***, driving the plot forward with unexpected developments that keep readers eagerly flipping pages.

The shifting magical laws also challenge familiar fantasy tropes, breaking away from traditional storytelling patterns. ***Readers are forced to reconsider their expectations*** and embrace the unknown, mirroring the characters' journeys of discovery within this magical realm. This departure from predictability adds depth and richness to the narrative, inviting readers to explore new possibilities alongside the characters.

By embracing unpredictability, *"The Grand Mage Wars"* encourages readers to engage actively with the story, anticipating what might happen next and reveling in the surprises. ***This surprise enhances reader anticipation and highlights the narrative's originality***, setting it apart from formulaic fantasy tales.

In a world where magic is ever-changing and unpredictable, characters must adapt and evolve in response to these shifting laws. This constant flux keeps readers invested in the characters' growth and development as they navigate challenges that arise from an unpredictable magical system. *The unpredictability adds complexity to character arcs,* pushing them beyond traditional roles and archetypes.

Ultimately, unpredictability catalyzes growth, both for the characters within *"The Grand Mage Wars"* and for the readers themselves. **By embracing the unexpected twists and turns of evolving magical laws**, readers are encouraged to think critically about the story's progression and engage with its themes on a deeper level. This immersive experience challenges preconceived notions about fantasy storytelling, inviting readers to embrace change and uncertainty as integral parts of an enchanting narrative.

The Evolving Magical Laws Framework

The concept of evolving magical laws within *"The Grand Mage Wars"* is encapsulated in a dynamic framework that illustrates the transformative nature of magic within the narrative. This Process Model is a roadmap for understanding how magical laws shift and adapt throughout the story, challenging familiar fantasy tropes and keeping readers engaged in the unfolding mysteries.

Initial State of Magical Laws

At the onset of the narrative, the magical laws are established with clear rules and limitations. These laws govern how magic operates within the world of the Grand Mage Wars, providing a foundation for characters to navigate their abilities and constraints.

Triggers for Change

Significant plot developments or characters' achievements trigger changes in magical laws. These events disrupt the established order, pushing magic into new realms and forcing characters to reevaluate their understanding of supernatural forces.

Narrative Milestones

Each shift in magical laws is linked to vital narrative milestones, driving the story forward and creating tension and suspense. These milestones mark pivotal moments where characters must adapt to evolving magical constraints or opportunities.

Character Responses

As magical laws evolve, characters must respond accordingly. They may develop new strategies for harnessing magic, seek out hidden knowledge to unlock untapped potential or confront unexpected consequences of these changes. These responses showcase personal growth and adaptation within the ever-changing magical landscape.

Unpredictability and Impact

Central to this framework is the element of unpredictability. The dynamic changes in magical laws enhance reader anticipation and investment in the storyline. By defying expectations and challenging traditional fantasy norms, these shifts keep readers on their toes and eager to uncover what lies beyond each twist in the magical system.

Visualization

A timeline or sequential flow diagrams could help readers visualize how these changes occur over time. By mapping out the chronological progression of evolving magical laws, readers can better grasp the cause-and-effect relationships that drive the narrative forward.

Reader Engagement

This framework aims to engage readers on a deeper level by highlighting the unpredictable nature of evolving magical laws. Encouraging them to reevaluate their expectations of fantasy storytelling invites them to embrace uncertainty and complexity to pursue a more immersive and thought-provoking reading experience.

Journey Through Enchantment: A Step-by-Step Exploration of Magical Evolution

The evolving magical laws in our narrative serve as a backbone for the unfolding drama and revolutionize the fabric of fantasy storytelling. This transformation keeps the plot fresh, and the readers engaged, constantly challenging their expectations and encouraging a deeper connection with the story.

Step 1: Familiarize yourself with the concept of evolving magical laws. Begin by embracing the idea that the rules governing magic are not static but fluid, reflecting changes that parallel the narrative's progression. This fundamental understanding paves the way for appreciating the depth and complexity of the story.

Step 2: Analyze the impact of evolving laws. Notice how these changes influence the storyline, shaping character decisions and plot twists. This dynamic approach to magical laws adds layers of anticipation, making each page a discovery rather than mere progression.

Step 3: Identify the rules and restrictions. Recognizing these elements is crucial as they dictate the strategies and interactions of characters within the story. Understanding these boundaries allows us to see how characters innovate and navigate challenges.

Step 4: Consider the consequences of the evolving laws. Reflect on how these shifts impact the characters and the world around them. Each change in the magical law introduces new challenges and opportunities, driving the narrative forward and weaving complexity into the tale.

Step 5: Reflect on the reader's experience. The unpredictable nature of these laws enriches the reading experience, injecting mystery and excitement into every chapter. This entertains and invites readers to think critically about the narrative structure and character development.

Step 6: Discuss the implications with fellow readers. Engaging in conversations about these evolving laws can deepen understanding and appreciation of the story's craftsmanship. Such discussions often reveal multiple interpretations and insights that enhance the enjoyment of the tale.

Step 7: Compare with other fantasy narratives. Examining how other stories handle similar concepts gives us a broader perspective on our narrative's unique approach to magical laws. This comparison highlights our story's originality and innovation in a tradition-rich genre.

These steps uncover the intricate dance of creativity and constraint that defines our magical landscape. This exploration deepens our appreciation of the narrative and underscores the significance of adaptability in both magic and storytelling. By challenging traditional tropes and embracing change, our tale stands as a beacon of originality, inviting readers to expect the unexpected and revel in the magic that evolves from within.

Chapter 7: Emotional Landscapes Unveiled

Can Power and Responsibility Coexist Peacefully?

In the dim light of early morning, Jonathan paced the length of his modest library, each step a silent testament to the turmoil brewing within him. The air was thick with the scent of old books, each leather spine a sentinel in the quiet. Today was not just another day; it was the day he would confront his sister about her recent claim to their father's estate. This claim threatened to tear their family apart.

He paused by the window, watching as the first light of dawn painted the garden in hues of gold and amber. His mind wandered to tales from *"The Grand Mage Wars,"* where characters like Merlin and Morganna navigated treacherous paths between power and responsibility. He wondered about their emotional depths, their personal motives, and how they might see his current predicament.

The sound of gravel crunching underfoot snapped him back to reality as his sister's car rolled into view. His heart hammered against his ribcage, not unlike the way Morganna must have when faced with choices that could alter the course of her life. Jonathan knew that today's conversation could very well change everything.

As he opened the door to greet her, memories flooded through him—childhood laughter echoing through halls now silent; secrets shared under starlit skies now overshadowed by this looming conflict.

He led her into the study, where dust motes danced in beams of light streaming through high windows.

They sat across from each other, an ocean of unspoken words stretching between them. Jonathan cleared his throat, his voice steady despite the storm.

"Sara," he began, *"do you remember how we used to imagine being powerful wizards like in our favorite stories? How did we believe that with great power came great responsibility?"*

She nodded slowly, her eyes reflecting a wariness born of sleepless nights and rehearsed arguments.

"I think," he continued, allowing himself a moment to choose his words with care as Merlin might have done when advising kings and knights, *"that what we are facing now is a test of those very ideals."*

Outside, a bird sang as if heralding a new beginning or mourning an end. The room seemed to hold its breath as Sara leaned forward slightly, her expression softening around edges hardened by legal battles and familial disputes.

Jonathan watched her intently, perhaps for the first time, understanding that this wasn't just about land or money but preserving something far more fragile—their bond as siblings.

As they delved deeper into the discussion, each argument laced with years of shared history and love despite their differences, Jonathan realized that perhaps there was room for power and responsibility in their hearts after all.

As they continue to navigate these treacherous waters fraught with personal motives and emotional depths, much like Merlin and

Morganna did centuries ago, will they find common ground, or will power corrupt them absolutely?

Unveiling the Hearts and Minds of Legends

In storytelling, the depth of a character's emotional journey can transform a simple narrative into a profound exploration of human nature and morality. This chapter delves into how *The Grand Mage Wars* achieves this transformation by meticulously unfolding the emotional landscapes of Merlin and Morganna. By focusing on their inner conflicts and motivations, the narrative invites readers to engage with the events and the very essence of what drives these characters.

The Emotional Core of Conflict

At its heart, every conflict is driven by emotion. This narrative takes us beyond the surface of magical battles and ancient rivalries to explore the ***emotional motivations*** behind each character's actions. By understanding Merlin's fears and Morganna's desires, we gain insights into their decisions, making them relatable and human. This approach enriches the story and deepens our connection to these legendary figures.

More Than Just a Plot Device

Characters are often merely seen as vessels to advance a plot. However, by integrating deep emotional layers, *The Grand Mage Wars* elevates its characters to be central elements in storytelling that resonate with readers on multiple levels. This method encourages us to reflect on our experiences and emotions, linking personal reflections to those of Merlin and Morganna.

Reflecting on Moral Values

This chapter encourages readers to contemplate complex moral questions through its characters' struggles and triumphs. What is the weight of power? How do responsibility and personal desire intersect? These are not just thematic elements; they stir a reflective journey among readers, prompting them to evaluate their own values against those depicted in the tale.

THE PSYCHOLOGICAL LATTICE

The intricate psychological makeup of each character does more than drive the plot—it paints a vivid picture of their psyche, which invites philosophical pondering. This depth ensures that the narrative isn't just consumed; it's experienced and internalized, offering a rich tapestry of insights that linger far beyond the final page.

Connection Through Reflection

By presenting characters with rich emotional depths, *The Grand Mage Wars* fosters a strong connection between readers and characters. This bond is cultivated through shared emotional experiences and reflections, making the fantastical elements more accessible and impactful.

Storytelling Enriched by Depth

Ultimately, this exploration of emotional landscapes does more than characterize; it enriches the entire fabric of storytelling. The reader is not merely an observer but becomes emotionally invested in the outcomes because they share in the emotional journeys of these characters.

As we proceed further into this discussion, we will explore how each layer of emotion enhances character relatability and elevates the overall narrative, making *The Grand Mage Wars a* compelling study of human emotion set against a backdrop of epic magical conflict.

In exploring the emotional motives and personal dilemmas of Merlin and Morganna, we uncover layers of complexity that enrich their characters beyond mere roles in a story. *Merlin*, the wise and powerful mage, grapples with the burden of his immense magical abilities and the responsibility of wielding such power. His internal struggles, often hidden behind a façade of calmness and wisdom, reveal a vulnerability that humanizes him and makes him relatable to readers facing challenges.

Morganna, on the other hand, embodies a different kind of complexity. As a character driven by ambition and a thirst for power, her motives are not always pure. However, delving into her past reveals a depth of emotion and trauma that shapes her actions in profound ways. By understanding her personal dilemmas, readers can empathize with her choices, even if they disagree with them.

The emotional landscapes of these characters serve as mirrors for readers to reflect on their own struggles, desires, and ethical boundaries. *Merlin's* internal conflicts with the consequences of his actions prompt readers to consider the weight of their decisions and their impact on others. *Morganna's* relentless pursuit of power raises questions about ambition, morality, and the lengths one is willing to go to achieve their goals.

Through the lens of emotional depth, *"The Grand Mage Wars"* transcends a simple tale of magic and conflict to become a narrative that challenges readers to confront their own values and beliefs. By presenting characters with rich emotional landscapes, the story invites introspection and self-examination, prompting readers to consider how they would navigate similar situations in their own lives.

Dive deeper into the emotional intricacies of Merlin and Morganna to uncover the moral dilemmas at the heart of "The Grand Mage Wars."

THE GRAND MAGE WARS: THE BATTLE OF LEGENDS UNFOLD

By delving into the emotional layers of Merlin and Morganna, readers are drawn into a world where characters are not just players in a grand narrative but complex beings with relatable struggles and desires. *These emotional depths bridge the story's fantastical setting and the readers' experiences, forging a connection that transcends mere entertainment.* Through understanding the personal dilemmas and motives of the characters, readers find themselves reflecting on their own values and beliefs, prompting introspection and contemplation.

Merlin and Morganna's emotional landscapes act as mirrors, allowing readers to see their own vulnerabilities, ambitions, and moral quandaries reflected back at them. This reflection fosters a deeper engagement with the story as readers empathize with the characters' choices and consequences. By witnessing the intricate interplay of emotions within the characters, readers are encouraged to explore their own emotional complexities and motivations, enriching their reading experience with a sense of shared humanity.

As readers connect with the emotional depth of the characters, they are invited to ponder universal themes such as power, responsibility, redemption, and sacrifice. The struggles faced by Merlin and Morganna resonate beyond the confines of the story, resonating with readers on a personal level. This resonance sparks contemplation on ethical dilemmas and philosophical questions that transcend time and place, inviting readers to confront their beliefs and values in light of the characters' journeys.

By exploring Merlin and Morganna's emotional landscapes, readers are prompted to consider how power can shape individuals and societies, leading to introspection on themes of ambition, integrity, and the consequences of one's choices. By weaving these emotional threads throughout the narrative, *"The Grand Mage Wars"* transforms from a mere tale of magic and conflict into a profound exploration of human nature and morality.

The emotional layers in the story not only deepen character development but also serve as conduits for reader reflection. By immersing themselves in the emotional turmoil of Merlin and Morganna, readers are compelled to confront their own fears, desires, and moral compasses. This introspective journey enhances the reading experience by offering a space for contemplation and self-discovery alongside the unfolding events in the magical realm.

As readers engage with the emotional landscapes unveiled in "The Grand Mage Wars," they are encouraged to navigate their inner worlds with empathy and understanding. The characters' struggles become mirrors for self-exploration, prompting readers to acknowledge their own vulnerabilities and strengths. Through this process of reflection, readers deepen their connection to the story and gain insights into their own emotional landscapes and personal growth.

By leveraging emotional depth in storytelling through characters like Merlin and Morganna, *"The Grand Mage Wars"* transcends traditional fantasy narratives to offer readers a transformative journey of self-discovery **where imagination meets introspection**.

The emotional richness woven into each character's arc serves as a beacon for readers to navigate their own complexities with courage and compassion. Through this exploration of deep-seated emotions and motives within characters and within oneself, readers embark on a profound quest to understand human nature in all its intricacies.

Analytical Framework: Emotional Landscapes Unveiled

Character Studies:

The first component of the framework involves in-depth character studies, focusing on the emotional motives and personal dilemmas of critical characters like Merlin and Morganna. Understanding their primary emotional drivers, such as ambition, fear, or loyalty, allows readers to connect with their inner struggles and complexities. By delving into these emotional depths, readers can empathize with the characters' decisions and transformations throughout the narrative.

Relationship Dynamics:

The next layer of analysis explores the relationships between characters and how emotional interplays shape their interactions.

By examining how emotions like trust, betrayal, love, or resentment influence character dynamics, readers gain insight into the complexities of human connections. These emotional bonds drive plot developments and reveal deeper truths about the characters' values and vulnerabilities.

Impact of Setting:

Another crucial element is the role of the setting and external circumstances in shaping characters' emotional landscapes. The backdrop of war, power struggles, and magical realms adds complexity to their emotions. Readers can see how external factors influence their internal struggles and decisions by contextualizing characters within these environments. This enriches the storytelling by providing a nuanced understanding of how surroundings impact emotional depth.

Visual Aids for Engagement:

Visual aids like emotional spectrum diagrams or character interaction maps can enhance reader engagement and visualization of emotional progression. These tools help readers track the evolution of emotions within characters and understand the interconnectedness between different emotional states. Visual representations offer a tangible way to grasp complex emotional journeys and deepen the connection with the narrative.

Encouraging Reader Reflection:

Ultimately, the framework encourages readers to reflect on their emotional responses to the characters' journeys. Readers can engage more deeply with the story's thematic resonance by prompting introspection on personal values, moral dilemmas, and emotional connections. This reflective process enriches the reading experience and invites readers to consider broader philosophical questions about power, responsibility, and human nature.

Overall Functionality:

The Analytical Framework is a roadmap for exploring the emotional landscapes unveiled in *"The Grand Mage Wars."* By dissecting character studies, relationship dynamics, setting impacts, and visual aids for engagement, readers can navigate the intricate web of emotions woven throughout the narrative. This structured approach fosters a deeper understanding of storytelling richness and relatability by highlighting the significance of emotional depth in character development and plot progression.

Exploring the Heart of the Tale

Emotional depth in storytelling is not just a tool; it's a bridge connecting the characters' experiences with our own. By delving into Merlin and Morganna's emotional motives and personal dilemmas, we've seen how their struggles and triumphs echo our own, making their journey feel both monumental and intimately personal. This approach does more than entertain; it invites us to *reflect on our values* and the complexities of our decisions.

The stories we cherish most are those that resonate with us on a personal level. Through the emotional landscapes of these characters, readers find a space for connection and reflection. It's a testament to the power of narrative to foster empathy and understanding. Each emotional layer peeled back reveals a new facet of human experience, urging readers to look inward and often discover aspects of themselves in the process.

Moreover, this emotional resonance significantly enhances storytelling's richness. When characters are relatable, their journeys matter more to us. The stakes feel higher, and their victories and defeats become ours. This makes the tale more gripping and rewarding, as we are emotionally invested in the outcomes.

In integrating these elements into our narrative, we've crafted a story and an experience—a journey that challenges, entertains, and enlightens. By focusing on these emotional dimensions, we ensure that our story does not merely pass through the minds of our readers but also touches their hearts.

As we move forward, let's carry the lessons learned from Merlin and Morganna's emotional odyssey. Let us remember that the simple, universal quest for understanding, acceptance, and connection is at the core of every epic tale. Herein lies the true magic of storytelling—a magic that is accessible to each of us, ready to be wielded wisely and with heart.

Chapter 8: Through the Lens of Legacy

When Legends Collide in the Mind of a Scholar

In the quiet corner of an ancient library, where the smell of old books lingered like memories too fond to let go, sat Eleanor. Her fingers traced the spine of a leather-bound tome, its gold lettering catching the dim light from a solitary window. Outside, the sun dipped low, casting long shadows across her notes scattered like leaves in autumn.

Eleanor's mind whirled with tales of Merlin and Morganna, those grand figures shrouded in myth and mystery. She was no stranger to their stories; they were old friends she revisited often, finding new paths in their legendary forests each time. Today, however, her task was different — not just to revisit but to compare, to dive deep into the myriad portrayals that spanned centuries.

A gust of wind rattled the window pane, pulling her momentarily from her thoughts. She glanced up, watching a lone bird fight against the breeze. It reminded her of Morganna — fierce and unyielding. Shaking her head slightly, Eleanor returned to her work. Her pen hovered over paper as she pondered how *"The Grand Mage Wars"* had reimagined these characters anew.

The book lay open beside her notes; its pages whispered secrets only she could hear. The author had dared to paint Merlin not as a wise old sage but a young rebel with a cause, his power still raw and untamed. Morganna was not merely an antagonist but a complex figure with motives as layered as the stories themselves.

Eleanor chewed on her lip lightly as she scribbled down comparisons. Each character's evolution through literature was not just academic; it felt personal as if she were charting the growth of old friends who had changed while she wasn't looking.

Her tea had gone cold beside her — untouched and forgotten in her zeal. The clock ticked away minutes like seconds lost in thought. How did these reinterpretations affect their legendary status? Did they enhance or diminish their essence?

As twilight deepened into the night and stars began to peek through the velvet sky outside, Eleanor leaned back in her chair. Her eyes roamed over lines filled with ink and ideas filled with life.

Could understanding these new layers alter our grasp on mythology itself?

Unlocking the Magic: A Comparative Exploration

As we delve into the rich tapestry of magical warfare woven throughout the annals of fantasy literature, few tales have captured the imagination as vividly as those of Merlin and Morganna. Their legendary conflict, replete with arcane spells and mythical beings, serves as an engaging narrative and a mirror reflecting the evolution of fantasy storytelling. In this exploration, we engage with these stories for their fantastical escapades and to deepen our understanding of how they inform and enrich contemporary works like *"The Grand Mage Wars."* Here, we dissect how comparative readings can amplify our appreciation of this book's unique position within the broader genre.

The allure of Merlin and Morganna's stories has always been their ability to blend the mystical with the human; their struggles are as much about power and ethics as they are about magic. By comparing these classic tales with *"The Grand Mage Wars,"* readers gain a multi-dimensional view of how traditional themes and motifs are being transformed in modern narratives. This chapter will guide you through a critical assessment of these transformations and innovations, highlighting what sets this work apart in the crowded realm of fantasy literature.

A New Lens on Legendary Tales

When we juxtapose *"The Grand Mage Wars"* with other stories from Merlin and Morganna's lore, we do more than revisit familiar scenes; we reframe them, gaining insights into the craft of storytelling itself. This comparative approach allows us to see the threads that connect classical mythology with today's fantasy writing, illuminating how authors weave old myths into new narratives that resonate with contemporary audiences.

This chapter promises to explore various interpretations of Merlin and Morganna's mythos, providing a backdrop against which "The Grand Mage Wars" can be critically assessed. We will explore how this novel reinterprets well-trodden paths and introduces innovative elements that refresh familiar themes—whether through complex character development, unexpected plot twists, or new magical laws.

The Evolution of Fantasy: From Then to Now

Understanding how fantasy narratives have evolved helps us appreciate the nuances that make each new story unique. *"The Grand Mage Wars"* does not exist in a vacuum; it is both a product of its literary predecessors and a response to them. This chapter will highlight elements where this novel diverges from traditional portrayals of magical conflicts, enriching the genre with fresh perspectives and creative approaches.

By engaging in this comparative analysis, we aim to enhance our enjoyment and understanding of modern fantasy narratives. It becomes clear that *"The Grand Mage Wars"* is not just another retelling but a significant contribution to the literary landscape, pushing boundaries and challenging readers to rethink what they know about magic, conflict, and resolution.

REFLECTING ON LEGACY

As we conclude our journey through magical realms, we must reflect on what makes *"The Grand Mage Wars"* stand out. This chapter serves as both a synthesis of critical themes explored throughout the book and an invitation to view these themes through a lens sharpened by historical insight and comparative critique.

Exploring this layered narrative approach encourages readers to enjoy and engage intellectually with the text. They are invited to see themselves as part of a larger conversation about what fantasy can be and what it can teach us about our own world.

In wrapping up our exploration, let us carry forward the lessons learned from Merlin and Morganna's timeless battles. Let these stories inspire us not just in their magical escapades but in their profound capacity to echo through ages, adapted by storytellers who understand that every generation needs its legends—told anew with wisdom from the past.

Comparative readings with other Merlin and Morganna tales can offer a rich tapestry of insights and perspectives that enhance our appreciation for *"The Grand Mage Wars."* By delving into various stories featuring these iconic characters, readers can uncover the nuances and unique approaches that set this book apart in fantasy literature. Each tale brings its own flavor and interpretation of magic, myth, and conflict, allowing us to see how *"The Grand Mage Wars"* stands out amidst a sea of narratives. **Comparative readings serve as windows into different worlds, each offering a fresh lens through which to view the complexities of the genre.**

Exploring Merlin and Morganna's myriad interpretations across different tales enriches our understanding. It showcases the innovative elements present in *"The Grand Mage Wars."* **By juxtaposing these characters against their traditional portrayals, readers can grasp the author's bold reinventions and creative liberties.** This exercise highlights the evolution of these legendary figures. It underscores the daring choices in weaving them into a new narrative tapestry. **We can appreciate the risks taken and the boundaries pushed in crafting a unique and captivating story** through comparison.

As we immerse ourselves in various Merlin and Morganna stories, we notice patterns, themes, and motifs that echo across different narratives. **These recurring elements serve as anchors that ground us in familiar territory while allowing for exploration into uncharted waters.** By recognizing these common threads and divergences, readers can better appreciate the genre's versatility and adaptability. **Each story adds a layer to our understanding, enriching our reading experience and broadening our perspective on classic characters.**

Through comparative readings, readers are encouraged to analyze and appreciate the nuances and complexities in *"The Grand Mage Wars."* **By drawing parallels with other tales, we can uncover hidden depths within the narrative, discovering layers of meaning and symbolism that might have otherwise gone unnoticed.** This exploration process fosters a deeper connection with the story, inviting readers to engage more profoundly with its themes and messages. **Comparative readings are a gateway to unlocking the full potential of "The Grand Mage Wars,"** revealing its intricacies and subtleties.

Continue Exploring Unique Approaches and Innovations

In *"The Grand Mage Wars,"* the approach to storytelling and the innovative elements woven into the narrative set it apart from traditional Merlin and Morganna tales. *The infusion of new perspectives, character development, and plot twists* elevates the book to a unique position within the fantasy genre. By critically assessing these unique approaches and innovations, readers can gain a deeper appreciation for the depth and creativity present in this captivating tale.

One notable aspect of "The Grand Mage Wars" is reimagining familiar characters. Rather than presenting Merlin and Morganna in a typical light, the author delves into their complexities, motivations, and inner struggles. This fresh portrayal adds layers of depth to these iconic figures, making them more relatable and intriguing to readers. *Humanizing these legendary characters* makes the story more immersive and emotionally resonant.

Another innovative feature of the book is the intricate world-building. The landscapes, magical systems, and political dynamics within *"The Grand Mage Wars"* create a rich tapestry for the characters to navigate. *The* author constructs a world that feels fantastical and authentic through vivid descriptions and meticulous attention to detail. This level of world-building enhances the reader's experience, allowing them to fully immerse themselves in the story.

The narrative structure of "The Grand Mage Wars" also sets it apart from traditional fantasy tales. The interweaving of multiple storylines, unexpected plot twists, and moral dilemmas keeps readers engaged and guessing at every turn. *This dynamic storytelling approach* adds a layer of unpredictability and excitement to the narrative, ensuring that readers are constantly on their toes.

Furthermore, the thematic explorations in "The Grand Mage Wars" delve into complex ideas such as power, destiny, redemption, and sacrifice. *By grappling with these universal themes,* the book transcends mere entertainment. It becomes a thought-provoking reflection on human nature and society. Readers are encouraged to ponder deeper questions about life, morality, and the consequences of one's actions.

Through its unique blend of character development, world-building, narrative structure, and thematic depth, *"The Grand Mage Wars"* is a shining example of modern fantasy literature. *By critically assessing these innovative elements,* readers can uncover hidden layers of meaning and appreciate the intricate craftsmanship that went into crafting this extraordinary tale.

APPRECIATING THE EVOLUTION of Modern Fantasy Narratives

A comparative reading of various Merlin and Morganna tales enriches our understanding of the genre. It highlights the unique innovations in *"The Grand Mage Wars."* By exploring different narratives, readers can gain a deeper appreciation for the evolution of modern fantasy literature and the distinctiveness of this particular book. *This comparative analysis allows us to see how storytelling styles have evolved, offering fresh perspectives on age-old characters like Merlin and Morganna.*

Through these comparisons, readers can uncover the intricate layers of storytelling techniques employed in "The Grand Mage Wars," showcasing how the book stands out amidst a sea of fantasy narratives. By critically assessing the unique approaches taken in this tale, readers can identify the creative nuances that set it apart from traditional Merlin and Morganna stories. *This process enhances our understanding of the book. It prompts us to reflect on the innovative ways classic characters can be reimagined.*

Appreciating the distinctiveness of modern fantasy narratives this book highlights encourages us to embrace change and new interpretations within the genre. As we delve deeper into the storylines and character developments in *"The Grand Mage Wars,"* we are reminded of the ever-evolving nature of fantasy literature and how each new interpretation adds to the rich tapestry of mythical storytelling. *By immersing ourselves in these narratives, we open ourselves to a world of imagination and creativity that transcends traditional boundaries.*

Reflecting on the evolution and distinctiveness of modern fantasy narratives allows us to see how far the genre has come and where it may be headed. By appreciating the innovations in *"The Grand Mage Wars,"* we can gain insights into how storytelling continues evolving, captivating audiences with its imaginative worlds and compelling characters. *This appreciation deepens our love for fantasy literature. It inspires us to seek out new stories pushing traditional tropes' boundaries.*

As we navigate through the realms of Merlin and Morganna stories, we are reminded of storytelling's power to transport us to magical worlds beyond our wildest dreams. *By embracing the evolution and distinctiveness of modern fantasy narratives, we honor the legacy of classic tales while paving the way for new adventures yet to unfold.*

Embarking on a journey through the vast realms of magical narratives enriches our understanding and appreciation of fantasy literature. By engaging in comparative readings of various tales featuring Merlin and Morganna, we uncover the rich tapestry that forms the backdrop of

The Grand Mage Wars. This approach deepens our grasp of the genre's evolution and accentuates the innovative elements that make this book stand out.

We discover a fresh perspective on a well-trodden path by critically assessing the unique approaches and innovations presented in this narrative. The exploration of new magical systems and the intertwining of known myths with unprecedented fantastical elements provide a captivating experience that is both refreshing and profound. It's clear that the evolution of modern fantasy narratives is vividly highlighted, showcasing a distinctiveness that can only be appreciated through such an immersive experience.

Reflecting on the themes woven throughout this book, from epic battles to the complex interplay between legendary characters, we see an expansive and intricately detailed world. This world captivates and entertains, drawing readers into a magical conflict that is as timeless as it is innovative. The journey through these pages is not just about following the clashes of Merlin and Morganna but also about understanding the depth and breadth of human imagination when it is allowed to run wild in fantasy.

This narrative encourages us to read, think, and feel deeply about the stories we encounter. It invites us into a dialogue with our past literary encounters, enriching those experiences with new insights and perspectives. Here lies the true magic of comparative reading—it does not merely highlight differences. Still, it builds bridges between the old and the new, enhancing our appreciation for both.

As we close this chapter on *The Grand Mage Wars*, let us carry forward the lessons learned and the joy experienced in this mythical exploration. May the enchantment of Merlin and Morganna's world inspire us to keep seeking new adventures in all the books we choose to explore next, always remembering that each page turned is a step into the vast, uncharted territories of our imaginations.

Epilogue

The Dawn of Peace: Reflecting on an Epic Tale

As we draw the curtains on this enchanting saga, it feels akin to stepping back from a vivid painting—the colors, emotions, and battles lingering in our minds like the afterglow of a sunset. In the concluding pages of our journey through magical realms, Merlin and Morganna have finally laid down their arms, not because one defeated the other but because they recognized the futility of eternal conflict. This realization wasn't merely about power but about understanding and harmony.

Throughout this tale, we've navigated through storms of chaos and whispers of peace, witnessing how even the mightiest forces must eventually seek balance. It mirrors our world's conflicts and resolutions—a perpetual reminder that peace often dwells in understanding our adversaries.

Applying Magic to Reality

Imagine wielding Merlin's wisdom or Morganna's strategic prowess daily. While we may not be casting spells, the essence of their magical abilities can inspire us to handle life's challenges with grace and creativity. *Adopting Merlin's wisdom could transform how we approach problem-solving,* turning every challenge into a puzzle to be solved with patience and thoughtfulness.

Similarly, Morganna's resilience reminds us that sometimes, persistence is necessary. Her ability to strategize can be mirrored in how we plan our careers or personal growth paths—always with foresight and adaptability.

Lessons Carved from Legends

This narrative was not just about battles fought with magic but also about each character's internal struggles—their desires, fears, and dreams. A dance of conflict and resolution pushed each character toward growth and realization. These are universal experiences echoing through every aspect of our lives.

Magic in this context is more than just fantasy; it's about ***the transformational power of self-belief and perseverance.*** Just as Merlin could summon winds or conjure light, we, too, can harness our inner strengths to illuminate dark times and move forward with gusts of passion.

Embracing Our Inner Mage

If there's anything you take away from this book, let it be the courage to face your battles with the dignity of Merlin and the cunning of Morganna. Each chapter you've turned mirrors a step where you faced something daunting yet emerged stronger.

I encourage you to reflect on these stories when faced with adversity. Remember that within you lies a grand mage ready to wield wisdom against ignorance and creativity against stagnancy.

Acknowledging the Unexplored

While this book has endeavored to cover vast terrains of magical lore, the realm of magic is boundless. Areas unexplored still whisper for attention—perhaps future tales will delve deeper into the mysteries untouched by Merlin and Morganna's journeys. The canvas remains wide open for new legends to paint their essence.

A Call to Forge New Legends

Let this story be more than a read; let it be a spark for your own adventures. Whether through writing, artistry, or your day-to-day endeavors, remember that you are part of this magical continuum—every choice and action weaving your thread into the larger tapestry of life.

As you turn this final page, do not see it as an end but as an invitation—a call to rise beyond what you know into what you can imagine.

"Magic exists who dare to believe."

May these words resonate within you as you forge into your own legends filled with magic and might—where every challenge is an opportunity for greatness.

Don't miss out!

Visit the website below and you can sign up to receive emails whenever Myrddin Sage publishes a new book. There's no charge and no obligation.

https://books2read.com/r/B-A-JBAOB-OHCHF

BOOKS 2 READ

Connecting independent readers to independent writers.

Also by Myrddin Sage

Echoes of the Ancient: Unlocking the Mysteries of Celtic Myth
Mythic Japan: Unlocking the Legends of Gods and Heroes
Echoes of Enchantment: Navigating the Magic of Celtic Mythology
Warriors and Wizards: The Heroes of Celtic Myth
Echoes of Valhalla: Unveiling the Modern Wisdom of Norse Myths
Gods Among Us: The Power and Intrigue of Roman Mythology
The Sword and the Sage: Unveiling the Truth of Excalibur and Merlin
Myth Unleashed: Rediscovering the Legends of Hercules and the Pantheon
Echoes of the Gods: Rediscovering the Heroes and Deities of Ancient Egypt
Ancient Echoes: Embracing Egyptian Wisdom in Our Modern World
Alexander the Great Uncovered: A Journey Beyond the Battlefield
Ghost Buster's Guide: The Truth Behind Paranormal Claims
The Grand Mage Wars: The Battle of Legends Unfold
The Grand Mage Wars: The Battle of Legends Unfold

About the Author

At 67, Myrddin Sage steps into the spotlight as a newly published author, bringing a tapestry of rich life experiences and a vibrant imagination. His journey from a Navy Veteran to a Retired Dispatcher of Messengers has endowed him with profound insights into human cultures and the natural world. As Myrddin introduces his debut novel, he shares a narrative infused with wisdom, whimsy, and a deep respect for the interconnectedness of life. Drawing on his academic background and extensive travels, Myrddin's work explores themes of adventure, discovery, and the transformative power of knowledge. With his first publication, he proves that new chapters can be embarked upon at any stage of life, inspiring readers with the message that it is always the right time to follow one's passions.

Milton Keynes UK
Ingram Content Group UK Ltd.
UKHW030853151124
451262UK00001B/197